# DON'T BE
## *LEFT BEHIND*

## James T. Harman

Joy Publishing
P.O. Box 9901
Fountain Valley, CA 92708
(714) 545-4521

BOOKSURGE

# DON'T BE LEFT BEHIND

Copyright © 2008, James T. Harman

Joy Publishing
P.O. Box 9901
Fountain Valley, CA 92708
www.JoyPublishing.com

BookSurge
7290-B Investment Drive
Charleston, SC 29418
www.BookSurge.com

ISBN: 0-939513-18-8

All Rights Reserved. We encourage the use of this material; however, in order to protect the contents from changes, neither this book, nor any part may be reprinted in any form without the written permission from the publishers, except for brief excerpts used in reviews whereby the reviewer may quote brief passages with proper credit.

All references from Scripture are from the King James Version unless noted otherwise.

Scripture quotations from the Thomson Chain Reference Bible, New International Version (NIV), Copyright 1973, 1978 and 1984 by International Bible Society.

Numerical references to selected words in the text of Scripture are from James H. Strong Dictionaries of the Hebrew and Greek words.

---

The picture of the beautiful bride with the veil on the cover is by Erica Koesler Copyright © 1997-2008 www.EricaKoesler.com

# Dedication

This book is dedicated to
My beautiful daughter Jennifer
Who has been such an inspiration
To her family and the many
People her life continues
To influence.

# Foreword

Most writers stay on safe ground and go with tradition, but Jim has taken the chance that few are willing to take. He has solid inspiration that allows him to take on one of the most entrenched traditions in the Church today.

My duty as a publisher calls for me to allow new insights to scripture to be investigated so they can be carefully examined by the full body of Christ. After reading this book I knew it had a new insight that was worth considering.

Some will find it hard to break with tradition, but others will find that this new insight answers for them lingering questions they have longed to have answered. As a publisher for nearly a quarter of a century very few manuscripts seem to have new material that cries out to be heard and considered. However, I felt the Spirit moving me to open up and give this new insight some prayer time before making a decision and hopefully you will do the same.

Enjoy having some of your traditional thinking challenged and feel the Holy Spirit move you to study your Bible to see if it is so (Acts 17:11).

Woody Young
Publisher

# Table of Contents

Foreword .................................................................. v
Prologue ................................................................... 9
Preface .................................................................... 11
Chapter  1 – Tradition ............................................... 13
Chapter  2 – Knowing the Timing ............................. 19
Chapter  3 – 70th Week of Daniel ............................. 27
Chapter  4 – Endtime Count of Days ........................ 35
Chapter  5 – Daniel's Clock About To Start Ticking? .. 45
Chapter  6 – God's Feast Days .................................. 55
Chapter  7 – Feast of Pentecost ................................. 65
Chapter  8 – Possible Coming Events ....................... 69
        False Peace? ............................................... 69
        Tabernacle Recovered? ............................... 70
        Midnight Cry? ............................................. 74
Chapter  9 – Abomination of Desolation ................... 77
Chapter 10 – Endtime Timeline ................................. 83
Chapter 11 – End of 7 Weeks? ................................... 89
Chapter 12 – Preparation For Days Ahead ................ 99

Epilogue .................................................................. 115
Reference Notes ...................................................... 117

Appendix A – Sign of Christ's Coming .................... 123
Appendix B – Of the Prophecy of the Seventy Weeks .. 129
        By Sir Isaac Newton
Appendix C – Outline of Book of Revelation ........... 137
Appendix D – Watching for Jesus ............................ 141
Appendix E – God's Feast Days ............................... 143

CHARTS:   # 1 – Length of Generation ................. 145
                # 2 – Endtime Timeline: 2009-2012 .... 149
                # 3 – Endtime Timeline: 2012-2015 .... 151
                # 4 – Endtime Timeline: 2009-2015 .... 153
                # 5 – Endtime Timeline: 2008-2011 .... 155
                # 6 – Endtime Timeline: 2014-2017 .... 157
Special Invitation .................................................... 159

# Prologue

Dear Christian Believer:

Back in the 1970's, I knew this world was moving into God's prophetic plan for Israel. I wanted to marry God's man, one that knew the Word, lived it, and had the Blessed Hope in his heart. Jesus heard my prayers and He most certainly sent me a very special husband. Before we met, somehow God breathed into my heart and filled me with the longing for His return. Through prayer and faith he gave me a rich and beautiful promise that He was going to use my spouse to let people know, at the end, of His coming.

I realized with the establishment of Israel in 1948, that this generation would be the one to witness the return of Christ and the time spoken of in Daniel 12:4 *"But, thou, O Daniel, shut up the words, and seal the book, even to the time of the end..."* I feel completely certain we are at this place in the history of the world and I whole-heartedly believe God has given Jim something important to do and say. This book, **DON'T BE LEFT BEHIND** could very well be the grand finale of God's purpose for his life. Please read it with a tender heart so that you will understand the rich blessings that can be found in the Living Word and the great promise to those with ears to hear: *"Go ye therefore into the highways, and as many as ye shall find, bid to the marriage."* (Matthew 22:9).

I encourage you to prayerfully read this most interesting study of the books of Daniel and Revelation. This book has the potential to invigorate your mind and heart with inspiring insight which will most certainly awaken your soul to the important message that this world is on the verge of momentous events.

While this book discusses many dates over the next several years, its purpose is not to set an exact date for when the Lord will return.

It is an honest attempt to help stir the hearts of God's people and to encourage them to dig deep in His Word and to seek His face, for the time of His return is so near. It is written for the sole purpose of preparing God's Church to rise up in holy faith and to pray to the Lord as we approach the final days.

Enjoy this study. It has the capacity to provoke your heart to wisdom and revitalize your soul with renewed faith. It could prove to provide the much needed insight which unlocks one of the grandest mysteries of the ages…the Return of our dear Savior.

**KEEP**
  **YOUR**
    **FIRE**
      **BURNING**

                       Love,

                       *Cindy Harman*

# Preface

After the Lord did not return, as many Christians had hoped, I went to the Lord and His Word with much prayer and fasting. So many things appeared to line-up and many fellow Watchmen were anxiously waiting for our Bridegroom to return.

The fact that Jesus has not returned must mean there is error in the way we are looking at things. After much searching and prayer, the Lord "Unveiled" my eyes to the one error that had been keeping me from seeing correctly. It was as if a light bulb went off and I could see for the very first time.

What you are about to discover (if you read this book) will go against the "Tradition" that almost every Bible student has been taught. Tradition has become so engrained in our thinking that when the truth is revealed the initial reaction is one of rejection and complete unbelief.

I strongly encourage everyone to approach this subject with an open mind and teachable heart that wants to know what God's wonderful Word has to show us. We all need to be like the Berean believers who were described in Acts:

> *"...were more noble than those in Thessalonica, in that they received the word with all readiness of mind, and searched the scriptures daily, whether those things were so."* (Acts 17:11)

Because of the "blindness" that "Tradition" has caused me, most of the Endtime Timelines that I have written about have been in error. I sincerely apologize to everyone and particularly to any individual who may have been harmed in their faith as a result. Our intentions have always been to encourage the Believers as we wait for our wonderful Lord and Saviour to return.

We also need to remember that:
> *"For now we see through a glass, darkly; but then face to*

> *face: now I know in part; but then shall I know even as also I am known."* (I Corinthians 13:12)

The lens through which we view the Scriptures is not perfect, but with the Holy Spirit's help we are sincerely seeking the truth that has been hidden as described by the Archangel Michael:

> *"But thou, O Daniel, shut up the words, and **seal the book**, even to the **time of the end**..."* (Daniel 12:4)

We strongly believe we are living in the ***"time of the end."*** The time for the book of Daniel to be unsealed has arrived, but before it can be unsealed the "blindness" created by "Tradition" must be corrected. Before Daniel can be unsealed, it first must be "Unveiled." The wise will understand and be ready. Don't be one of those Left Behind.

# Chapter 1 – Tradition

Paul gives us a strong warning about "Tradition" as shown in the following translations of Colossians 2:8:

> *"Beware lest any man **spoil you** through philosophy and vain deceit, after the **tradition of men**, after the rudiments of the world, and not after Christ."* (KJ)

> *"See to it that no one **takes you captive** through hollow and deceptive philosophy, which depends on **human tradition** and the basic principles of this world rather than on Christ."* (NIV)

> *"See that no one shall be **carrying you away** as spoil **through the philosophy** and vain deceit, according to the deliverance of men, according to the rudiments of the world, and not according to Christ."* (Young)

Tradition is a philosophy created by man and its effect can be to spoil us and to take us captive. It can even carry us away as a spoil!

Paul warns all Christians: *"Study to shew thyself approved unto God, a workman that needeth **not to be ashamed, rightly dividing the word of truth.**"* (II Timothy 2:15)

Tradition can create a teaching that appears to be correct, but if it has not been *"rightly divided"* then it can cause us to be ashamed. As described in the Preface to this book, I certainly am ashamed for any harm that I may have caused because of my teaching *"after the tradition of men."* Again, I am very sorry if I have ever hurt anyone's faith in the Lord or in His Word.

## PRE-TRIB RAPTURE

The first major "Tradition" that I had to apologize for was back in 1991. At that time, I had written books on the subject of the Rapture and I strongly believed in the traditional teaching taught by most prophecy teachers. The traditional view says that when Jesus returns, all Christians will be Raptured before the Tribulation period begins. This is the view held by most Believers living in the Church today, but sadly it is based upon man's tradition and not what the Word of God has to say.

In 1991, the Lord showed me that not all Believers will be taken at first but that there will be a separation between the wise and foolish virgins (Matthew 25:1-10). Those Firstfruit Believers who are found in the Church of Philadelphia (and a few of those in Sardis) will be taken to be with the Lord before the Antichrist is revealed. The remaining Lukewarm Believers who are found in the Church of Laodicea will be **Left Behind** to face their time of testing.

As a result of shedding the Traditional view, the Lord had us produce the book entitled: ***The Coming Spiritual Earthquake.*** A PDF version of this book is available for free by going to our Website: www.ProphecyCountdown.com

"NO ONE KNOWS THE DAY OR HOUR"
The next Tradition that the Lord helped me shed was the one based upon a verse in Matthew:

> *"But of that day and hour knoweth no man, no, not the angels of heaven, but my Father only."* (Matthew 24:36)

The Traditional teaching on this subject says that we are not to know when Jesus will return and we should not concern ourselves with it. This Tradition will be discussed in great detail in the next chapter. We are to know when the Lord returns and we should be actively watching for that great day.

"70th WEEK OF DANIEL"
The Traditional teaching on the 70$^{th}$ Week of Daniel is firmly implanted in the vast majority of Christians today. This teaching

has been so engrained in our minds that it is hard to imagine how it could be wrong.

Chapter 3 of this book will examine this Tradition in detail. It will be shown that we have been "Blinded" to what the Scriptures are really saying. It has taken most of the Church *"Captive"* and *"Carried Us Away"* into error that can make us all ashamed for not *"rightly dividing the word of truth."*

Arthur Bloomfield once shared the following insight:

*"The only defense against false teaching is truth...(and)...false doctrine is like a disease germ; it sets up a mental block to truth. A person once infected is very difficult to reach. Its seems as if one simply cannot get through to him."*

Traditions are created and then handed down as if they are sound biblical doctrine. The Traditional teaching on the 70$^{th}$ Week of Daniel is based upon the following verse in Daniel:

> *(27) And he shall confirm the covenant with many for one week: and in the midst of the week he shall cause the sacrifice and the oblation to cease, and for the overspreading of abominations he shall make it desolate, even until the consummation, and that determined shall be poured upon the desolate."*
> (Daniel 9:27)

The Traditional teaching says that the Antichrist will arrive on the scene and confirm a 7 Year Peace Treaty, but after 3 ½ Years he will break the Treaty and then put an end to the Sacrifices that the Jewish people are making in their re-built Temple. This is popularly called the "70$^{th}$ Week of Daniel" and literally hundreds of books have been published on this one verse of Scripture.

Breaking from this Traditional teaching is very hard. One wants to hold onto it so dearly because it has been taught so widely that to think otherwise sounds impossible. How could one verse of Scripture be so wrongly understood?

Without an open mind and teachable spirit, it is next to impossible to allow the Holy Spirit the opportunity to teach us. We can become so steeped in human tradition, that we can't even hear what God's Word is saying to us. Jesus warned us of this in Mark 7:13:

> *"Thus you nullify the word of God by your tradition that you have handed down. And you do many things like that."* (Mark 7:13 NIV)

Tradition can actually nullify the word of God! The King James version says, *"rendered the Word of God of no effect."* By listening to and by following tradition, we can entirely miss what God is saying to us in His Word.

Tradition is like spiritual quicksand, pulling all its victims deep into its dark depth. Satan can use Tradition to keep people from the truth of God's Word. This can be extremely dangerous for the Church. We can become so sure of ourselves and of our own position that we actually are led astray. In Bloomfield's **Before the Last Battle Armageddon** he cautions us: *"If the usual interpretation...should fail...many people would almost lose their faith."*

Indeed, if our life is based upon a teaching that will prove wrong, there is great danger of loosing ones faith. A good example relates to the teaching that all Christians will be taken when the Rapture occurs as discussed previously. Since this is not what the Word of God teaches, and most in the Church believe they will be taken, what will happen to their faith once the Rapture takes place and they are left behind?

It is time for the entire body of Christ to wake-up and examine their own beliefs in line with what God's Word actually says. May we all pray for the Holy Spirit to give us open hearts that are teachable to what He wants to show us. May we be careful not to follow the traditions of the past if they do not line-up with what the Word of God actually says:

*"Dear Lord, give us all the ability to discern what the truth of your Holy Word has to say to us. Give us ears that will listen and hearts that will understand. In Jesus name we pray. Amen."*

# Chapter 2 – Knowing The Timing

## RELIGIOUS SPRIIT

Whenever a date for the Lord's return is set, the first objection that most people make is, "You can't know the DAY or the HOUR, therefore let's not even discuss it." The argument goes on to say that it is wrong to discuss dates and that no one knows when Jesus is coming.

Let's be careful that we are not like the Pharisees and Sadducees who were rebuked by Jesus himself in Matthew 16:2-3:

*"When it is evening ye say, "It will be fair weather; for the sky is red." And in the morning, "It will be foul weather today: for the sky is red and lowring." O YE HYPOCRITES, ye can discern the face of the sky; but can ye not discern the SIGNS OF THE TIMES?"*

The religious leaders at the time of Christ were rebuked because they could not discern the time that they were living in. Had they read the Scripture with a proper heart, they would have known the TIME they were living in and they would have known to be LOOKING for their Messiah. In a similar manner, we are currently living at a time when the Scriptures are SHOUTING: JESUS IS COMING! Unfortunately, not everyone has the "ears to hear" or the "eyes to see" what is transpiring before them.

Because of the tradition that we can not know about the timing of Endtime events, many people will be caught off guard when Endtime events begin to take place.

## DAY AND HOUR

To ensure that we are not rebuked by Jesus, let's take a better look at what the Word of God has to say about knowing the timing.

The most widely used verse people quote when they want to prove that we are not to know when Jesus is returning is found in Matthew: *"But of that day and hour knoweth no man, no, not the angels of heaven, but my Father only."* (Matthew 24:36)

What most people fail to remember, however, is the preceding verse: *"Heaven and earth shall PASS AWAY, but my words shall not pass away."* (Matthew 24:35)

The day and hour that no one knew about when Jesus spoke those words was when heaven and earth will pass away at the end of the 1,000 year Millennium. The timing of when this will occur is found in Revelation 21:1:

> *"Then I saw a new heaven and a new earth, for the first heaven and the first earth HAD PASSED AWAY."*

The reason that this time is not known is found in Revelation 20:3, which says Satan is let out of the bottomless pit at the end of 1,000 years for: *"a LITTLE SEASON."* No one but God knows how long Satan will have to deceive the nations at that time.

## HOUR YOU THINK NOT

The next objection to knowing the timing of end time events is related to the following verses in Matthew 24:42-44:

> *"WATCH therefore: for YE KNOW NOT WHAT HOUR your Lord doth come. But know this, that if the GOODMAN of the house had known in what WATCH the THIEF would come, he would not have suffered his house to be broken up. Therefore be ye also ready: for in such AN HOUR AS YE THINK NOT the Son of man cometh."*

# Knowing The Timing

On the surface of things, it appears that the Lord is coming as a THIEF and at a time we will not know. For the answer to this, we need to turn over to the parallel passage in Luke where Peter asks the Lord a very vital question in Luke 12:39-41:

> *"And this know, that if the Goodman of the house had known what hour the thief would come, he would have watched, and not suffered his house to be broken through. Be ye therefore ready also: for the Son of Man cometh at AN HOUR WHEN YE THINK NOT."*

> *"Then Peter said unto him, LORD, SPEAKEST THOU THIS PARABLE UNTO US, OR EVEN TO ALL?"*

In this parallel passage concerning when the Lord is going to return, Luke records a very important question that Peter asks: Is this parable for US, meaning fellow believers, or for everyone? Before we look at the Lord's answer, let's remember why the Lord spoke in **parables:**

> *"...Why do you speak to them in **parables**? He replied, "The knowledge of the secrets of the kingdom of heaven has been given to you, but not to them."* (Matthew 13:10&11)

> *"Unto you it is given to know the mystery of the kingdom of God: but unto them that are without, all these things are done in parables: That seeing they may see, and not perceive; and hearing they may hear, and not understand."* (Mark 4:11&12)

Jesus used parables, because not everyone is given knowledge to the mysteries of the kingdom. Peter's question about who Jesus meant in the parable of not knowing about the timing becomes an essential point.

Now, let's see what the Lord's answer is to this crucial question:

*"And the Lord said, Who then is that **FAITHFUL** and **WISE** steward, whom HIS lord shall make ruler over his household, to give them their portion of meat in due season.""Blessed is **THAT** servant, whom his lord when he cometh shall find so doing. Of a truth I say unto you, that he will make him ruler over all that he hath."*

*"But and if that servant say in his HEART, My lord delayeth his coming; and shall begin to beat the menservants and maidens, and to eat and drink, and to be drunken; The lord of that servant will **COME IN A DAY WHEN HE LOOKETH NOT** for him, and at **AN HOUR WHEN HE IS NOT AWARE**, and will cut him in sunder, and will appoint him his portion with the unbelievers."*
(Luke 12:42-46)

First of all, Jesus says that the **FAITHFUL** and **WISE** steward will be greatly blessed. They are dressed and READY with their lamps burning brightly WAITING and WATCHING for their Lord to return (see Luke 12:35 & 36 and Matthew 25:10).

But notice what the **UNFAITHFUL** servant is thinking in his heart: *"My lord delayeth his coming."* He is **not** LOOKING and WATCHING as the faithful and wise steward is. Instead, he is beating (Greek: wounding the conscience) of his brothers and sisters. He is saying: NO ONE KNOWS when the Lord is coming, so let's forget about it and talk about something else; let's concern ourselves with this present time and enjoy ourselves.

Because of the attitude of the unfaithful servant's heart, Jesus says that he comes for him: *"in a DAY when he LOOKETH NOT FOR HIM, and at an HOUR WHEN HE IS NOT AWARE."* **To the unfaithful servant** Jesus is **coming like a thief**. He is going to take him by surprise on a DAY AND HOUR that he will not expect Him.

The wise and faithful servant will be ready, waiting and watching for Jesus, while the unfaithful servant will not know and will be taken by surprise.

## THIEF IN THE NIGHT

This teaching that the wise and faithful will know and the unfaithful will not know is also confirmed for us by Paul:

> *"Now, BROTHERS, about times and dates we do not need to write to you, for you know very well that the day of the Lord will come LIKE A THIEF in the night. While people are saying, "Peace and safety," destruction will come on THEM SUDDENLY, as labor pains on a pregnant woman, and they will not escape."* (I Thessalonians 5:1-3)

Most people stop reading at the end of the third verse to try to prove their point that the Lord is going to come as a THIEF. He is coming like a THIEF, but to whom is He coming to as a THIEF? Notice what Paul says in the fourth verse: *"But you, BROTHERS, are not in darkness so that this DAY SHOULD SURPRISE you like a THIEF."*

Paul is saying that the Lord's coming should not surprise the Christian (BROTHER). While the rest of the world will be surprised like a THIEF, the true Christian SHOULD NOT be surprised.

This confirms what Jesus was teaching us in His parables. The wise and faithful steward will be READY, WAITING and WATCHING for Him when He comes for them. The unfaithful and foolish servant will not be looking for Him and will be taken by surprise.

## LOOKING FOR JESUS

Further evidence for this teaching is found in the book of Hebrews. Hebrews 10:25 shows that the faithful servant will, "SEE THE

DAY APPROACHING." How could we see the day coming if we are not supposed to know? By simple implication, we should know.

Not only should we know, but more importantly we should be LOOKING for Him as taught to us in Hebrews 9:28:

> *"So Christ was once offered to bear the sins of many; and UNTO THEM that LOOK FOR HIM shall he appear the second time without sin unto salvation."*

This makes it quite clear, Jesus is returning the second time for those who are LOOKING FOR HIM (see Appendix D). Looking for Jesus is an attitude of the heart that longs to be with the Bridegroom. Those Believers who fail to be looking are in great peril.

The book of Revelation implies the faithful will know when the Lord is coming:

> *"I know your deeds; you have a reputation of being alive, but you are dead. WAKE UP! Strengthen what remains and is about to die...Remember, therefore, what you have received and heard; obey it, and repent.*
>
> *BUT IF YOU DO NOT WAKE UP, I will come LIKE A THIEF, and you will NOT KNOW at WHAT TIME I will come to you."* (Revelation 3:2-3)

The church of Sardis was dead. The Lord rebuked it and warned it to repent and to wake up. By implication, if this church will only obey His admonition, they will not be surprised like a thief and they will KNOW the TIME.

The Word of God is very clear. The wise and faithful servant will be looking for Jesus and they will be ready, waiting and watching for Him. They will know the time and will not be taken by surprise.

The unfaithful and foolish servant will not know when Jesus returns and they will not be ready for Him. They will be taken by surprise like a thief and they will not know the day or hour when He will return. The choice is left up to the individual. He can heed the Word of God and be looking for the soon return of Jesus, or else he can continue listening to the tradition of not knowing and be taken by surprise like a thief.

## KNOW IT IS NEAR

Finally, Jesus commanded us to KNOW the timing of end time events: *"Now learn a parable of the fig tree; When his branch is yet tender, and putteth forth leaves, ye know that summer is nigh: So likewise ye, when ye shall see all these things, KNOW THAT IS NEAR, EVEN AT THE DOORS."* (Matthew 4:32-33)

Just prior to telling us the fig tree parable, Jesus listed all of the signs that we would see, such as: wars and rumors of wars, nation rising against nation, famines and earthquakes in diverse places. These signs were just the beginning of birth pains, indicating that the time for delivery (Tribulation period) was just about due.

Then Jesus gives us one of the most important clues to knowing His return is near. He tells us to LEARN a parable or lesson about the FIG TREE. Most bible students agree that the Fig Tree represents the nation of Israel (See Hosea 9:10 and Joel 1:6-7).

Until this century, Israel had been scattered throughout the world with no land to call home. Then on May 14, 1948, the state of Israel was founded and on May 15, 1949, was recognized by the United Nations. Then on June 7, 1967, Israel recaptured the Old City of Jerusalem. The importance of this one event will be discussed later in this book when the Endtime Timelines are discussed.

The important point is that Jesus tells us once we see the nation of Israel established again we can and SHOULD KNOW that His return is near, even at the DOOR! When someone knocks on your door or rings the door bell, what do you do? Of course, you get up, and go to the door. Jesus was telling us that once we see all the signs converging on the world scene, AND we see Israel established as a nation, we are to KNOW that He is as close as the front door. In other words, it is time to get up, get ready, Jesus is ALMOST HERE!

WISE WILL UNDERSTAND

The book of Daniel ends with words that are prophetic for the time we now live:

> *"Go your way, Daniel, because the words are closed up and sealed UNTIL the TIME OF THE END. Many will be PURIFIED, made SPOTLESS and REFINED, but the wicked will continue to be wicked. None of the wicked will understand, but THOSE WHO ARE WISE WILL UNDERSTAND."* (Daniel 12:9-10)

May Daniel's words resonate in the reader's ears as they continue in this book. Many will be PURIFIED and made SPOTLESS and the WISE WILL UNDERSTAND.

# Chapter 3 – 70<sup>th</sup> Week of Daniel

CHAPTER 9 OF DANIEL

As mentioned previously, the Traditional teaching on the 70<sup>th</sup> Week of Daniel is based upon this one verse in Daniel 9:27:

> *"And he shall confirm the covenant with many for one week: and in the midst of the week he shall cause the sacrifice and the oblation to cease, and for the overspreading of abominations he shall make it desolate, even until the consummation, and that determined shall be poured upon the desolate."* (Daniel 9:27)

The Traditional teaching says that the Antichrist will arrive on the scene and confirm a 7 Year Peace Treaty, but after 3 ½ Years he will break the Treaty and then put an end to the Sacrifices that the Jewish people are making in their re-built Temple. This is popularly called the "70<sup>th</sup> Week of Daniel" and literally hundreds of books have been written on this one verse.

After you finish reading this section, you will hopefully see that the above interpretation is like a fairy tale compared to the real truth that God has for us.

To properly understand this prophecy in Daniel, I suggest that the reader review the entire 9<sup>th</sup> chapter of the book of Daniel. Some of the major highlights are include below:

> *"(2) In the first year of his reign I, Daniel, understood by books the number of the years, whereof the word of the LORD came to Jeremiah the prophet, that he would accomplish seventy years in the desolations of Jerusalem. (3) And I set my face unto the Lord God, to seek by prayer and supplications, with fasting, and sackcloth, and ashes: (4) And I prayed unto the LORD my God, and made my confession, and said, O Lord, the great and dreadful God, **keeping the covenant and mercy to them***

*that love him, and to them that keep his commandments;"*

Daniel begins by saying that he came to understand *"by books"* i.e., the writings of Moses and the Prophets, the teachings on the Captivity of his people, the Jews. From the book of Jeremiah, Daniel understood that the Babylonian Captivity was to last seventy years (see Jeremiah 25:11 and Jeremiah 29:4-10). The Prophet Daniel was a devout student of Bible Prophecy. He knew the Scripture and he sought the Lord for understanding. Because of Daniel's devotion, the angel Gabriel was sent to him:

> *"(20) ¶ And whiles I was speaking, and praying, and confessing my sin and the sin of my people Israel, and presenting my supplication before the LORD my God for the holy mountain of my God; (21) Yea, whiles I was speaking in prayer, even the man Gabriel, whom I had seen in the vision at the beginning, being caused to fly swiftly, touched me about the time of the evening oblation. (22) And he informed me, and talked with me, and said, O Daniel, I am now come forth to give thee skill and understanding. (23) At the beginning of thy supplications the commandment came forth, and I am come to shew thee; for thou art greatly beloved: therefore understand the matter, and consider the vision."*

Gabriel was sent by the Lord to give Daniel the answer to his prayer. Gabriel's answer is found in the last four verses of Chapter 9, upon which hundreds of books have been written:

> *"(24) Seventy weeks are determined upon thy people and upon thy holy city, to finish the transgression, and to make an end of sins, and to make reconciliation for iniquity, and to bring in everlasting righteousness, and to seal up the vision and prophecy, and to anoint the most Holy." (25) Know therefore and understand, that from the going forth of the commandment to restore and to build Jerusalem unto the Messiah the Prince shall be seven weeks, and threescore and two weeks: the street shall be built again,*

> *and the wall, even in troublous times. (26) And after threescore and two weeks shall Messiah be cut off, but not for himself: and the people of the prince that shall come shall destroy the city and the sanctuary; and the end thereof shall be with a flood, and unto the end of the war desolations are determined.* ***(27) And he shall confirm the covenant with many for one week: and in the midst of the week he shall cause the sacrifice and the oblation to cease, and for the overspreading of abominations he shall make it desolate, even until the consummation, and that determined shall be poured upon the desolate."***
> (Daniel 9:24-27)

The very last verse which is highlighted (v.27) is the key verse that has been misinterpreted and misunderstood by most in the Church. Notice that the verse says, *"he shall confirm the covenant with many..."* The questions we need to ask ourselves are "who is the 'he' that Daniel is referring to and what is the 'covenant with many'?"

We need to remember that this prophecy is dealing with Daniel's prayer:

> *"And I prayed unto the LORD my God, and made my confession, and said, O Lord, the* ***great and dreadful God****, keeping* ***the covenant*** *and mercy to them that love him, and to them that keep his commandments;"* (Daniel 9:4)

The first thing we notice is the fact that Daniel mentioned in his prayer before God that He is the **great God** who keeps the **covenant** to those that love him. In the NIV version of verse 4 it reads:

> *"O Lord, the* ***great and awesome God****, who* ***keeps his covenant of love*** *with all who love him and obey his commands,"* (Daniel 9:4 NIV)

Yes, the covenant that Daniel is referring to is the covenant of love and mercy that God made to His people.

Notice what Jesus had to say regarding this covenant at the Last Supper:

> *"And he said unto them, This is my blood of the **new testament (covenant)**[1242] which is **shed for many**."*
>
> (Mark 14:24)

At the Last Supper, the Lord was revealing how the wine the Disciples were about to partake represented the blood of the new covenant. This shows that His blood actually strengthens the original covenant because there would no longer be any need to continue to offer sacrifices to God. His act of love and obedience on the cross made the original covenant a more durable covenant that would permanently bind His love to mankind.

What did Daniel say of the covenant in Daniel 9:27:

> *"(27) And he **shall confirm (strengthen)**[1396] the **covenant with many**..."*

Isn't this exactly what Jesus said that His blood would do? By shedding His own blood, Jesus strengthened the covenant of love and mercy that God had previously bestowed upon His people who love and obey His commands. By obediently going to the cross, Jesus shed His own blood to strengthen the covenant for many who will come to believe.

The precious life blood of Jesus Christ is like superglue that forever binds God's covenant of love and mercy to mankind. It creates an everlasting bond of God's love that can never be broken (see Hebrews 7:22-28).

At this point it is extremely important to point out that this prophecy in Daniel beautifully pictured how God sent his only son Jesus Christ to fulfill mankind's ultimate redemption. Through human "Tradition" Satan has twisted and perverted this Holy Scripture to mean that the "he" in Daniel 9:27 is the Antichrist! This grand deception has blinded mankind from the beautiful truth God originally meant for this passage.

## ONE WEEK

Now let's look at the next part of the verse:

> *"And he shall confirm the covenant with many **for one week: and in the midst of the week he shall cause the sacrifice and the oblation to cease**,* (Daniel 9:27)

The original intention that God had for the Jewish people was the offer of the Kingdom. God sent His son Jesus Christ, however the Jews rejected Him and after 3 ½ years of His ministry on this earth, they had the Romans crucify Jesus on the cross. This verse is showing that God sent Jesus for what would have been for 7 years (one week) but because of their hardness of heart and unbelief they rejected Jesus and had Him killed.

Daniel then says, *"and in the midst of the week he shall cause the sacrifice and oblation to cease..."* After 3 ½ years of ministry, Jesus death on the cross forever ended God's requirement for man to offer animal sacrifices as atonement for sin. Jesus death on the cross literally caused the **"sacrifice and the oblation to cease"** forever more. Jesus paid the penalty for sin forever to all who will acknowledge Him by confessing Him as their own personal Saviour.

Daniel's **prophecy Clock** immediately stopped ticking when Jesus died on the cross. In God's eyes there will never be any need for animal sacrifices again. Jesus paid it all and sacrifices are no longer required. Daniel's final week or final 7 year period began when Jesus was baptized. His ministry lasted for a period of approximately 3 ½ years or in the "midst of the week." Daniel's **Clock** has stopped half way through the final week.

There only remains about 3 ½ years until the end of this last week. In other words, Daniel's prophecy only has 3 ½ years to go. There is no 7 year Tribulation period remaining!

## 7 YEAR TRIBULATION PERIOD

The "Traditional" interpretation of Daniel says:

70<sup>th</sup> Week of Daniel = Tribulation Period = 7 years

The Word of God does not mention a 7 year Tribulation Period. The only one Scripture that does mention a 7 year period is Daniel 9:27! The *"one week"* of Daniel 9:27 has already elapsed 3 ½ years with the ministry of Jesus. The first half of Daniel's final week has already been fulfilled!

There are several places in the Word of God that do mention a period of 3 ½ years. Let's review each of them:

|  |  | Daniel's 70<sup>th</sup> Week | |
|---|---|---|---|
| Reference | Time Period | 1<sup>st</sup> Half | 2<sup>nd</sup> Half |
| Daniel 7:25 | 42 months |  | x |
| Daniel 12:7 | 42 months |  | x |
| Revelation 11:2 | 42 months |  | x |
| Revelation 11:3 | 1,260 days |  | x |
| Revelation 12:6 | 1,260 days |  | x |
| Revelation 12:14 | 42 months |  | x |
| Revelation 13:5 | 42 months |  | x |

The above summary is very enlightening. It appears that each of the above references is referring to a period of approximately 3 ½ years. There is not one Scripture that says there is a 7 year period of time remaining.

By distorting Daniel 9:27, human "Tradition" has created a doctrine that a 7 year Tribulation Period is coming in the future before Jesus returns. This grand deception has created almost a fairy tale for all who are captivated by its scheme. This author believed and taught this distortion and has humbly repented before the Lord for allowing this error to carry him astray by not rightly dividing the Word of Truth.

The time of the Tribulation Period is rapidly approaching, however, there is no 7 year period mentioned in Scripture. The first half of Daniel's 70$^{th}$ week has been completed by our wonderful Lord and Saviour Jesus Christ.

# Chapter 4 – Endtime Count of Days

DANIEL AND REVELATION

In the previous chapter we discovered that both the books of Daniel and Revelation provide various counts of days relating to the Endtimes. The purpose for this book is not to set an exact date for any Endtime event. However, we need to remember that we are living in the *"time of the end"* and that the prophecies in Daniel are to be *"unsealed"* at that time and that the *"wise will understand."* The foolish and the scoffers will not understand and they will tell you that it is wrong to discuss dates. That is why the foolish will be taken by surprise!

The purpose of this section is to review the 7 major Counts of Days outlined in the Scriptures and to ascertain what events may be described and discuss possible fulfillments. (These numbers ①②③…etc. will be used in the **Endtime Timelines** found later in this book).

① GENTILES ON TEMPLE MOUNT (42 MONTHS)

The first time period we will discuss is found in Revelation 11:

> *"(1) And there was given me a reed like unto a rod: and the angel stood, saying, Rise, and **measure the temple** of God, and **the altar**, and them that worship therein. (2) But **the court which is without the temple leave out**, and measure it not; for it is **given unto the Gentiles**: and the holy city shall they **tread under foot forty and two months.**"*
> (Revelation 11:1-2)

The above Scripture provides a great deal of insight into events about to take place during the coming Tribulation Period.

First of all notice that the angel is instructed to measure the temple and the altar which is somehow separated or divided by an area that is given to the Gentiles. This suggests that the Jewish people will negotiate some form of sharing arrangement over the Temple Mount. Rumors have been circulated that such a scenario is being discussed, and the Word of God seems to indicate that some arrangement may be reached that will initially allow the Jewish people to share the Temple Mount with the Gentiles. Also notice at the end of verse 2, it states Jerusalem (holy city) is *"****tread under foot** for **42 months**."* What this may mean will be discussed in Section ③ below.

## ② 2 WITNESSES (1,260 DAYS)

The next time period is found in the very next verse of Revelation 11:

> *"(3) And I will give power unto my two witnesses, and they shall prophesy a **thousand two hundred and threescore days**, clothed in sackcloth."* (Rev. 11:3)

This indicates that God will send His 2 witnesses who will be given power to witness and prophesy for 1,260 days. The identity of these 2 witnesses has been speculated for years by many prophecy students. Most believe they will be either Enoch and Elijah or Moses and Elijah. Their actual identity will not be resolved in this study since the main point is to show that God will send 2 witnesses who will be given great power during the final Endtime events:

> *"(5) And if any man will hurt them, fire proceedeth out of their mouth, and devoureth their enemies: and if any man will hurt them, he must in this manner be killed. (6) These have power to shut heaven, that it rain not in the days of their prophecy: and have power over waters to turn them to blood, and to smite the earth with all plagues, as often as they will. (7) And **when they shall have finished their testimony**, the **beast** that ascendeth out of the bottomless pit shall make war against them, and shall overcome them, and **kill them**."* (Revelation 11:5-7)

This indicates that the 2 Witnesses will finish their 1,260 days of testimony and then the beast (Antichrist) will kill them. This beast will be discussed in Section ⑥ below, but after the Antichrist kills the 2 Witnesses notice what happens:

> *"(8) And their dead bodies shall lie in the street of the great city, which spiritually is called Sodom and Egypt, where also our Lord was crucified. (9) And they of the people and kindreds and tongues and nations shall see their dead bodies **three days and an half,** and shall not suffer their dead bodies to be put in graves. (10) And they that dwell upon the earth shall rejoice over them, and make merry, and shall send gifts one to another; because these two prophets tormented them that dwelt on the earth."*
>
> *"(11) ¶ And **after three days and an half** the Spirit of life from God entered into them, and they stood upon their feet; and great fear fell upon them which saw them. (12) And they heard a great voice from heaven saying unto them, **Come up hither. And they ascended up to heaven in a cloud;** and their enemies beheld them. (13) And the same hour was there a great earthquake, and the tenth part of the city fell, and in the earthquake were slain of men seven thousand: and the remnant were affrighted, and gave glory to the God of heaven. (14) **The second woe is past;** [and], behold, the **third woe cometh quickly."***
> (Revelation 11:8-14)

The 2 Witnesses end their 1,260 days of testimony and are then killed by the Antichrist in the city of Jerusalem. Their bodies will lie in the street for 3 ½ days and after that period of time they will be Raptured into heaven for the whole world to see! The Scripture then indicates that the $2^{nd}$ Woe is past with the $3^{rd}$ and final Woe to follow very quickly thereafter.

(Note to reader: See Appendix C for an Outline of the Book of Revelation to help understand the sequence of events.)

③ DAILY SACRIFICES (1,290 DAYS and 2,300 or 1,150 DAYS)

The daily sacrifices are mentioned in several places in Daniel and Revelation. Let's begin our review in Daniel 12:

> *"(11) And from the time that the daily sacrifice shall be taken away, and the abomination that maketh desolate set up, there shall be a thousand two hundred and ninety days."* (Daniel 12:11)

As we discovered in Chapter 3, the requirement for daily sacrifices came to an end when Jesus became the ultimate sacrifice for all of mankind. In God the Father's eyes, His son Jesus Christ paid the penalty for everyone's sins and the daily sacrifices will never be required again.

At the crucifixion of Jesus, Daniel's **prophetic Clock** in Daniel 9:27 **stopped ticking**. The prophetic Clock is about to be started again in the very near future **and once it begins ticking again** Daniel 12:11 states there will be a **period of 1,290 days** until the *"abomination that maketh desolate"* or what many refer to as the "abomination of desolation." This "abomination of desolation" will be covered in greater detail later in this book. Suffice it to say for now, Daniel 12:11 indicates once the **prophetic Clock** starts ticking again, there will be a period of 1,290 days until the abomination takes place.

In addition to this period of 1,290 days in Daniel 12:11, Daniel also mentions a period of time of "2,300 evenings and mornings" in Daniel 8:

> "8 *And it waxed great, even to the host of heaven; and it cast down some of the host and of the stars to the ground, and stamped upon them. 11 Yea he magnified [himself] even to the prince of the host, and by him the **daily sacrifice was taken away**, and the **place of his sanctuary was cast down**. 12 And an host was given [him] against the daily [sacrifice] by reason of transgression, and it cast down the*

> *truth to the ground; and it practised, and prospered.*
>
> *13 ¶ Then I heard one saint speaking, and another saint said unto that certain [saint] which spake,* **How long shall be the vision concerning the daily sacrifice, and the transgression of desolation,** *to give both the sanctuary and the host to be* **trodden under foot?** *14 And he said unto me,* **Unto two thousand and three hundred days;** *then shall the sanctuary be cleansed."* (Daniel 8:10-14)

The New International Version as well as several other versions notes that the period of time is 2,300 evenings and mornings leading many bible students to conclude that Daniel is referring to a period of 1,150 actual days (2,300 / 2):

> *"He said to me, "It will take 2,300 evenings and mornings; then the sanctuary will be reconsecrated."*
> (Daniel 8:14 NIV)

Whether Daniel 8:14 is referring to 2,300 days or 1,150 days is not known for 100% certainty. We will use this information later on in this book when final **Endtime Timelines** are developed, and both counts of days in Daniel 8:14 could be meaningful.

Resumption of Daily Sacrifices?

While God no longer requires animal sacrifices, the Jewish people do not understand this as Paul noted in Romans 11:25:

> *"For I would not, brethren, that ye should be ignorant of this mystery, lest ye should be wise in your own conceits; that* **blindness in part is happened to Israel,** *until the fullness of the Gentiles be come in."* (Romans 11:25)

The Jews have been blinded[1] to the sacrifice Jesus made for them. The religious leaders in Israel still believe that they need to rebuild the Temple and offer animal sacrifices once gain. While these sacrifices are not required by God, the Jewish people's blindness may cause them to attempt animal sacrifices once again.

If this does occur, this could be part of the explanation for the various Scriptures that seem to indicate daily sacrifices are taking place in the Endtime. In a later chapter in this book, we will look at possible scenarios for how this could take place. Suffice it to say for now, the Scriptures appear to reveal that some form of sanctuary for animal sacrifices may stand on the Temple mount as described by Ezekiel:

> *"He measured it by the four sides: it had a wall round about, five hundred [reeds] long, and five hundred broad, to **make a separation** between the **sanctuary** and the **profane place.**"* (Ezekiel 42:20)

Ezekiel comments appear to line up with what we discovered in Revelation 11:1-2 above.

> *"(1) And there was given me a reed like unto a rod: and the angel stood, saying, Rise, and **measure the temple** of God, and **the altar**, and them that worship therein. (2) But **the court which is without the temple leave out,** and measure it not; for it is **given unto the Gentiles**: and the holy city shall they **tread under foot forty and two months.**"* (Revelation 11:1-2)

Outside of the "temple & altar" the "**court**" is described as the "**profane place**" which indicates that the Dome of the Rock (profane place given to the Gentiles) could be standing alongside the place where the Jews institute animal sacrifices once again. If so, both Revelation 11:2 and Daniel 8 indicate that Jerusalem will be *"trodden under foot"* once again. The sanctuary was destroyed in 70 AD as Jesus predicted and Endtime events indicate Jerusalem will witness much turmoil in the days ahead.

> **Revelation 11:2** *"But the court which is without the temple leave out, and measure it not; for it is given unto the Gentiles: and the **holy city** shall they **tread under foot** forty and two months"* (42 Months)
>
> **Jerusalem** is trodden down by the Gentiles for **42 Months**

> **Daniel 8: 11, 13-14** *"11 the daily sacrifice was <u>taken away</u>, and the place of his sanctuary was <u>cast down</u> 13…How long shall be the vision concerning the daily sacrifice, and the transgression of desolation, to give **both** the **sanctuary** and the **host** to be **trodden under foot**? 14 And he said unto me, **Unto two thousand and three hundred days**; then shall the **sanctuary be cleansed.**"* (1,150 or 2,300 Days)
>
> **Daily sacrifices are <u>taken away</u>** and **Sanctuary** is **<u>cast down</u>**.
>
> **Sanctuary and host** (army?) are trodden down for **1,150 Days** or **2,300 Days** and then **Sanctuary is cleansed**.

## ④ ISRAEL INTO WILDERNESS (1,260 DAYS & TIME, TIMES & ½ TIME)

Revelation 12 shows that Israel will be driven into the wilderness for a period of 1,260 days:

> *"And there appeared a great wonder in heaven; a **woman** clothed with the sun, and the moon under her feet, and upon her head a crown of twelve stars:"* (Revelation 12:1) (Also see Genesis 37:9)

> *"And the **woman fled into the wilderness**, where she hath a place prepared of God, that they should feed her there **a thousand two hundred and threescore days**."*
>
> (Revelation 12:6)

This flight into the desert is also described a little later on in the same chapter:

> *"And to the **woman** were given two wings of a great eagle, that she might fly into the wilderness, into her place, where she is nourished for **a time, and times, and half a time**, from the face of the serpent"* (Revelation 12:14).

Notice that in this second description Israel appears to be airlifted into the wilderness and the period of time mentioned is not an exact count of days as the previous flight into the wilderness. The second flight into the desert is for a period described as a time (one year), and times (2 years) and half a time ( ½ year) or a period of 3 ½ years. The <u>first</u> flight is an exact count of 1,260 days while the <u>second</u> flight is for a period of about 3 ½ years (which many mean it could be slightly less than or more than 1,260 days),

### ⑤   CHRISTIANS PERSECUTED (TIME, TIMES & ½ TIME)

In our book entitled: ***The Coming Spiritual Earthquake*** we show that not all of the Church will be Raptured before the Antichrist is revealed. Only the Firstfruit Believers will be taken at first and the remaining Lukewarm church of Laodicea will be **Left Behind** to face the trials of the Tribulation Period.

> *"And he shall speak great words against the most High, and shall wear out the **saints of the most High**, and think to change times and laws: and they shall be given into his hand until **a time and times and the dividing of time**."*
>
> (Daniel 7:25)

As mentioned in the previous section, *a time and times and the dividing of time* represents a period of 3 ½ years. This indicates that the Antichrist *"he"* mentioned above will have a period of 3 ½ years to *"wear out the saints of the most High"*. This length of time is very similar to the time given to the Antichrist in the following section.

### ⑥ ANTICHRIST POWER (42 MONTHS)

> *"And there was given unto him a mouth speaking great things and blasphemies; and **power was given unto him** to continue **forty and two months**."* (Rev. 13:5)

The Antichrist is given power to rule for a period of 42 Months. This is a period of about 3 ½ years but may not be exactly 1,260 days.

### ⑦ PROMISED BLESSING (AFTER 1,335 DAYS)

The final time period in this section is the 1,335 days found in the last chapter of the book of Daniel:

> *"Blessed is he that waiteth, and cometh to the thousand three hundred and five and thirty days."* (Daniel 12:12)

This is the last count of days found in the book of Daniel. Daniel indicates that whoever reaches the end of these 1,335 days will be blessed.

# Chapter 5
# Daniel's Clock About to Start Ticking?

Most people who study the Endtime prophecies in Daniel are familiar with the concept that there is a time gap of close to 2,000 years between the weeks that were fulfilled when Jesus walked the earth and the time when the Endtime period is about to begin. In essence, Daniel's **prophetic Clock** stopped ticking when Jesus died but it will start again at some future point in time.

TIMES OF THE GENTILES

One of the key prophecies that indicate we are living in what Daniel called: *"the time of the end"* is the prophecy relating to the re-establishment of Israel:

> *(24) And they shall fall by the edge of the sword, and shall be **led away captive into all nations**: and **Jerusalem shall be trodden down of the Gentiles**, until the **times of the Gentiles be fulfilled**.*
>
> *(29) ¶ And he spake to them a parable; Behold the **fig tree**, and all the trees; (30) When they now shoot forth, ye see and know of your own selves that summer is now nigh at hand. (31) So likewise ye, when ye see these things come to pass, know ye that the kingdom of God is nigh at hand. (32) Verily I say unto you, **This generation shall not pass away, till all be fulfilled.*** (Luke 21:24, 29-32)

The first part of Luke 21:24, indicates that Israel will be dispersed into all the nations. This prophecy was fulfilled on August 5, 70 AD when Jerusalem was destroyed and the Jewish people were led away into captivity from the land God originally gave to them. Because of their hardness of heart and their blindness to the truth Jesus had for them, they became a nation without a homeland until 1948.

Then in June 1967, the Arabs attacked Israel with the hope of driving the Jewish people from their land. During this 6 day war, Israel recaptured the Old City of Jerusalem on June 7, 1967. From August 5, 70 AD until this date, Jerusalem had been under the control of the Gentiles. June 7, 1967 marked a major **Prophetic Milestone** because Jerusalem was no longer under Gentile rule.

Jesus indicates in Luke 21:29-32 that the generation to witnesses the establishment of the *"fig tree"* will not pass away until everything in the prophecies have been fulfilled. The *"fig tree"* represents the nation of Israel (See Hosea 9:10 and Joel 1:6-7). In other words, Jesus is telling us that once we see these events take place we are to know for certain that our redemption is drawing very near.

> *"(28) And when these things begin to come to pass, then look up, and lift up your heads; for your redemption draweth nigh."* (Luke 21:28) [2]

The next logical question to ask is: how long is a generation? Speculation on this issue has been quite abundant. As the old TV show used to say: "That's the $64,000 question."

Some of the most recent estimates have included the following:

| 1948 | 1948 | 1949 | 1950 | 1951 | 1967 |
|------|------|------|------|------|------|
| 40   | 50   | 50   | 50   | 50   | 40   |
| 1988 | 1998 | 1999 | 2000 | 2001 | 2007 |

The above chart may seem silly to some, but not to those who are looking for the Blessed Hope:

> *" (12) Teaching us that, denying ungodliness and worldly lusts, we should live soberly, righteously, and godly, in this present world; (13) **Looking for that blessed hope**, and the glorious appearing of the great God and our Saviour Jesus Christ;"* (Titus 2:12-13)

The Bride of Christ is longing for the day to be with her Bridegroom. She does not fit in with this present world where Satan is the *"prince of the power of the air"* (Ephesians 2:2).

Whenever a possible time passes by without the Rapture taking place, the Bride is temporarily saddened, but she continues to press on in her watch for she knows that her wonderful Bridegroom won't be one day late for their important wedding day.

## JERUSALEM – MAJOR KEY

As stated earlier, the recovery of Jerusalem on June 7, 1967 was a major Prophetic key that Jesus is about to return.

Since Jerusalem is such an important part of solving our question about the length of a generation, I decided to go back to the time that Jerusalem was destroyed. Jesus had predicted its destruction before he was killed:

> *"(1) And as he went out of the temple, one of his disciples saith unto him, Master, see what manner of stones and what buildings are here! (2) And Jesus answering said unto him, Seest thou these great buildings?* **there shall not be left one stone upon another, that shall not be thrown down.***"* (Mark 13:1-2)

> *"As for these things which ye behold, the days will come, in the which there shall* **not be left one stone upon another***, that shall not be thrown down."* (Luke 21:6)

This prophecy was fulfilled by the Roman army who destroyed the second Temple on the $10^{th}$ of AV in 70 AD. This day fell on August 5, 70 AD.

## MINISTRY OF JESUS

At this point I wondered how long the generation was that witnessed this prophetic event being fulfilled. Those people living in 70 AD were actually witnessing a major prophecy that Jesus had predicted would take place! I then realized that I needed to determine when Jesus actually began his public ministry.

In order to understand the time of Jesus' public ministry we need to know either a starting date or an ending date. The ending date has been well documented in a book entitled: ***The Coming Prince*** by Sir Robert Anderson. While I no longer believe all his conclusions are valid or correct, he has documented the actual week that Jesus died. Anderson shows that Jesus entered the city of Jerusalem on Palm Sunday on April 6, 32 AD. Most chronologies use this date as a milepost, however, the day Jesus entered Jerusalem is not the starting or ending point related to Daniel's prophecy:

> *"And he shall confirm the covenant with many **for one week: and in the midst of the week he shall cause the sacrifice and the oblation to cease**,* (Daniel 9:27)

The key date in this prophecy is the day Jesus died. This is the day which brings and end to Daniel's prophetic Clock in the *"midst of the week"* or about ½ way through this final 7 year period. Since Jesus rode into Jerusalem on April 6, 32 AD which was a Sunday, Jesus died on Wednesday which would have been April $9^{th}$. Tradition says that Jesus died on Friday, but that would have been impossible for Him to be resurrected on Sunday. (See the Passover Fulfilled by Jesus in Chapter 6).

Now that we have the ending date for Jesus' ministry, we need to back up a certain number of days to determine when our Lord started His ministry.

Passovers
The book of John records 4 Passover that Jesus kept. These were:

| | |
|---|---|
| John 2:13 | Spring 29 AD |
| John 5:1 | Spring 30 AD |
| John 6:4 | Spring 31 AD |
| John 13:1 | Spring 32 AD |

# Daniel's Clock About to Start Ticking? 49

The above period of time represents approximately 1,080 days. To this number we would have to add time for His baptism, for His temptation by Satan, the calling of his disciples, and his first miracle at the wedding in Cana. We do not know for certain how long these events would have taken, so we need to estimate possible lengths of time that it could have taken.

We know that Daniel 9:27 says Jesus died in the midst of the 7 year period. This 7 year period would translate into 2,520 days (7 x 360 = 2,520 days).

For Jesus to die in the midst of this period of time we can make the following estimates for purposes of our analysis:

    Scenario ①    1,185  (2,520 less 1,335)
    Scenario ②    1,260  (2,520 less 1,260)
    Scenario ③    1,335  (2,520 less 1,185)

Since there is no way to know for 100% certainty how long it took from the time Jesus was baptized in the Jordan river until His first Passover in the Spring of 29 AD, the above estimates are close approximations of the time in question.

The estimates summarized above were then entered in the very top of Chart # 1 that can be found in the back of this book. It is entitled: ENDTIME CALCULATIONS – Length of Generation.

## LENGTH OF GENERATION

The next step is to subtract the estimated number of days in our Lord's ministry from the date we know Jesus died on: April 9, 32 AD.

This calculation gives us 3 estimated dates that Jesus may have started His ministry:

    Scenario ①                  January 9, 29 AD
    Scenario ②                  October 26, 28 AD
    Scenario ③                  August 12, 28 AD

With the above starting dates, we can now determine the length of the generation that was alive when Jesus lived that were witnesses to the destruction that He prophesied would take place. As discussed at the beginning of this chapter, the Jewish Temple was destroyed on August 5, 70 AD. This was the 10$^{th}$ of AV which is a key prophetic day in the history of the nation of Israel. Both the 1$^{st}$ and 2$^{nd}$ Temples were destroyed on this day and several other significant events have also occurred on this day (see Chapter 6).

In the very middle of Chart # 1, we show the calculations of subtracting August 5, 70 AD from the above three dates for when Jesus started His ministry and determine the possible length of the generation that witnessed the Temple's destruction:

    Scenario ①      15,184 Days or 42 Years
    Scenario ②      15,259 Days or 42 Years
    Scenario ③      15,334 Days or 42 Years

## GENERATION TO WITNESS MESSIAH'S RETURN

As discussed earlier in this chapter, the major prophetic milestone of the Recovery of the Old City of Jerusalem took place on June 7, 1967 *"(24) And they shall fall by the edge of the sword, and shall be led away captive into all nations: and **Jerusalem shall be trodden down of the Gentiles**, until the **times of the Gentiles be fulfilled"*. (Luke 21:24)

The first part of the above prophecy took place when Jerusalem was destroyed in 70 AD and the nation of Israel was forced away to all the nations. The second part of this prophecy relates to the present time when mankind has witnessed the miraculous recovery of Jerusalem from Gentile control in 1967. The very bottom of Chart # 1 shows the calculations for possible times for re-starting Daniel's **prophetic Clock**:

    Scenario ①      January 1, 2009
    Scenario ②      March 17, 2009
    Scenario ③      May 31, 2009

Chart #1, shows three possible times that Daniel's **prophetic Clock** could start ticking again:

> Scenario ①        January 1, 2009
> Scenario ②        March 17, 2009
> Scenario ③        May 31, 2009

Let's review when Daniel's prophetic Clock stopped:

> *"And he shall confirm the covenant with many **for one week**: **and in the midst of the week he shall cause the sacrifice and the oblation to cease**,* (Daniel 9:27)

Daniel says *"and in the midst of the week he shall cause the sacrifice and oblation to cease..."* After 3 ½ years of ministry, Jesus death on the cross ended God's requirement for man to offer animal sacrifices as atonement for sin. Jesus death on the cross literally caused the **"*sacrifice and the oblation to cease.*"**

Daniel's **prophetic Clock** immediately stopped ticking when Jesus died on the cross. Daniel's final week or final 7 year period began when Jesus was baptized. His ministry lasted for a period of approximately 3 ½ years or in the *"midst of the week."* Daniel's **prophetic Clock** has stopped half way through the final week.

We know that at some future time the clock is going to start ticking once again. The above three dates are presented as possible times for the prophecies to be set in motion for the final fulfillment of Daniel's last 3 ½ year period.

<u>42 YEARS</u>
It is interesting to note that the above three dates all indicate a final period of 42 years since Israel recaptured Jerusalem. Is 42 a significant number in relationship to being the length of the Final Generation?

The first book we published dealing with the Lord's return was entitled: ***The Blessed Hope.*** In that book we discussed why the number 42 could be very significant in relation to the Lord's coming. A few pertinent excerpts are included below:

"In Ed Vallowe's excellent book, **Biblical Mathematics** he outlines every significant number in the bible and gives a detailed analysis of each number's meaning. What appeared very interesting was his analysis of the number 42:"

"Forty-two is the number that is associated with **Israel' Oppression**, and the **Lord's Advent** to the earth; both His first and second coming."

"In Matthew 1:17, FORTY-TWO generations are divided into three periods of FOURTEEN generations each. THREE is the number for RESURRECTION and FOURTEEN is the number for DELIVERANCE...3 multiplied by 14 makes FORTY-TWO, the number of the fullness of time spoken in Galatians 4:4"

"Our Lord's SECOND ADVENT to the earth will also be associated with the number FORTY-TWO. At the end of the FORTY-TWO months of Israel's oppression by the beast, Christ makes Hid SECOND ADVENT to the earth. (See II Thes. 2:8, Rev. 13:5, Rev. 11:2, Rev. 12:40 and Daniel 12:7)"

"Our Lord's return to the earth at the end of the FORTY-TWO months of the reign of the beast must not be confused with His appearing...to catch away His (watching) saints. In II Kings 2:23-25, we have the incident when two she bears came out of the woods, and tare FORTY and TWO children. Here the little children were the infidel young men of Bethel who were worshippers of the golden calf instead of Jehovah."

"It was God who sent the bears, and we have to believe that the offenders were worthy of such judgement. The term, "bald head" had no special reference to the lack of hair, according to some authorities; it signified a worthless fellow. It was a term of contempt. Here it was equal to blasphemy of God for the young men mocked Elisha as a prophet of Jehovah, in contemptuous allusion to the translation of Elijah, which they no doubt denied and made fun of. The idea it seems to be, "Go up (be translated) like Elijah, you worthless fellow?"

"Here again, FORTY-TWO is associated with the coming of Christ or the translation of the Saints that shall take place at the Rapture or first phase of the Second Coming. This number (42) is used FOURTEEN times in the Bible which reveals the DELIVERANCE of God's people at the Coming of Christ."

"Was God giving His faithful a key to the time He is coming back? Is the length of a generation that Jesus referred to in Matthew 24, somehow connected to 42 years?"

The fact that Israel will have taken control of Jerusalem from the Gentiles for a period of 42 years since 1967, could be highly significant for the year 2009.

We need to remember that Israel lost their $2^{nd}$ Temple 42 years after Jesus started His public ministry. From that time until 1967, Jerusalem was in the hands of the Gentiles. As of 2009, Israel will have recovered her sacred city for 42 years, but we know that Israel will loose Jerusalem again during the Endtimes:

> "... to give **both** *the* **sanctuary** *and the* **host** *to be* **trodden under foot**?" (Daniel 8:14)
>
> "... *and the* **holy city** *shall they* **tread under foot** *forty and two months*" (Revelation 11:2)
>
> "*And the* **woman fled into the wilderness**, *where she hath a place prepared of God, that they should feed her there* ***a thousand two hundred and threescore days***." (Rev. 12:6)

Both the sanctuary and the city of Jerusalem will be trodden down once again and Israel will be forced to flee into the wilderness for a period of 3 ½ years.

If Daniel's **prophetic Clock** is about to be re-started, 2009 (5769 on Hebrew Calendar) could be the time for it to start ticking. While the $42^{nd}$ year appears to be somehow related to the start of

2009, we must also take note of the fact that the 42$^{nd}$ anniversary of the recapture of the Old City of Jerusalem will take place on June 7, 2008. If Daniel's **prophetic Clock** is about to start ticking again, the time for it to begin could be at hand.

# Chapter 6 – God's Feast Days (Shadows of Things to Come)

> *"Surely the Sovereign Lord does nothing without revealing his plan to his servants the prophets."* (Amos 3:7 NIV)

The Lord has a plan for mankind and He communicates that plan to us through His Holy Word. He then reveals that plan to His servants the prophets.

Before Jesus departed from this earth he comforted His disciples with these words:

> *"(12) I have yet many things to say unto you, but ye cannot bear them now. (13) Howbeit when he, the Spirit of truth, is come, he will guide you into all truth: for he shall not speak of himself; but whatsoever he shall hear, that shall he speak: and **he will shew you things to come.**"*
> (John 16:12-13)

Jesus promised the disciples that he would send the Holy Spirit to guide us into all truth and to show us things to come. God has given us His precious Word that has the answers for how we should live and how we should prepare for the time ahead. As outlined in Chapter 4 of this book, He has provided us with a multitude of counts of days and months that outline some of the events that are about to take place in the near future.

We need to be careful, however, because Peter cautions us that Scripture is not for one's private interpretation:

> *"(19) **We have** also a **more sure word of prophecy;** whereunto ye do well that ye **take heed**, as unto a light that shineth in a dark place, until the day dawn, and the day star arise in your hearts:*
>
> *(20) Knowing this first, that no **prophecy of the scripture is of any private interpretation.** (21) For the prophecy came*

> *not in old time by the will of man: but holy men of God spake as they were moved by the Holy Ghost."*
>
> (II Peter 1:19-21)

The wonderful Word of God was written by men moved by the Holy Spirit and Jesus said the Holy Spirit would be sent to guide us into all truth and show us what is to come.

## 70th WEEK OF DANIEL

As we have discovered so far in this book, the 70th Week of Daniel is not some future period of 7 years that will be started by a Peace Treaty that the Antichrist confirms and then breaks 3 ½ years later. This is a human Tradition that has been handed down as Biblical Truth. We now know that ½ of Daniel's 70th Week has already been fulfilled by the ministry of Jesus Christ. There only remains a 3 ½ year period for Daniel's 70th Week to be completed.

This revelation requires a paradigm shift in how we approach our analysis of the time that remains to be fulfilled. The purpose of our analysis is not to set and EXACT date for any Endtime event. However, once these Endtime events are set in motion, the final count of days have been given to us in the books of Daniel and Revelation. As we noted at the beginning of this chapter, the Holy Spirit had this information recorded by Holy men of God so that God's people living in the Endtime would know what to expect. To ignore this knowledge would be not be very wise:

> **"My people are destroyed for lack of knowledge**: *because thou hast rejected knowledge, I will also reject thee, that thou shalt be no priest to me: seeing thou hast forgotten the law of thy God, I will also forget thy children."* (Hosea 4:6)

## GOD'S FEAST DAYS

Several good books[3] have been written and the Internet is filled with Christian websites that go into great detail to describe how

# God's Feast Days

God set the Feast Days as divine appointments that He has made in the past and will make in the future.

These Feasts are controlled by the orbits of the sun, moon, and earth and the Hebrew calendar is regulated to keep track of the Feasts.

God has ordained these special days and various Endtime events are scheduled to occur on or near these appointments.

In developing the **Endtime Timelines** found in the back of this book, I used the counts of days discussed in Chapter 4 and compared them to God's Feast Days from 2007 to 2017. Excel spreadsheets were used to analyze hundreds of Feast Days over this time period. An interesting pattern emerged when the Endtime Count of Days were compared to the Feast Days. Six of the Timelines examined showed a correlation between the Feast of Pentecost in the Spring and the Fall Feasts of either Tabernacles or Atonement:

| **Pentecost** | **Fall Feasts** |
|---|---|
| 5/31/2009 | Atonement – 9/26/2012 |
| 5/27/2012 | Atonement – 9/23/2015 |
| 6/15/2008 | Tabernacles – 10/12/2011 |
| 5/23/2010 | Tabernacles – 9/19/2013 |
| 6/12/2011 | Tabernacles – 10/09/2014 |
| 6/08/2014 | Tabernacles – 10/05/2017 |

Pentecost
Most Bible students are aware that the Feast of Pentecost always falls on a Sunday and is always 50 days after the Feast of First Fruits. In the next Chapter we will look into the Feast of Pentecost in more detail to see why it is the one Feast day that the Rapture of Firstfruits Believers may be scheduled for. The Holy Spirit came 50 days after the resurrection to empower and anoint Believers for

the ministry of the Church. We believe the Lord could remove those anointed Believers who are *"filled with the Holy Spirit"* on this same Feast. An entire chapter will be devoted to this very important Feast day.

We also know that the Antichrist is getting ready to make his appearance on the world scene; but before he is revealed the Lord will Rapture His Firstfruit Believers. The timing of this Firstfruit Rapture and the appearance of the Antichrist could take place on the same day and the Feast of Pentecost is a very likely time.

Atonement

The Day of Atonement is also called Yom Kippur and it falls on the $10^{th}$ of Tishri. In 1973, the Arabs attacked Israel on this day named the Yom Kippur War, but God miraculously intervened and saved Israel from being annihilated.

This Feast day is one of the holiest days of the year and it is a day of **mourning** for one's sins. When Jesus Christ returns to fight the final battle of Armageddon, the Jewish people will **mourn** like never before when they realize it was Jesus who they had killed:

> *"(1) This is the word of the LORD concerning Israel. The LORD, who stretches out the heavens, who lays the foundation of the earth, and who forms the spirit of man within him, declares: (2) "I am going to make Jerusalem a cup that sends all the surrounding peoples reeling. Judah will be besieged as well as Jerusalem. 3 On that day, when all the nations of the earth are gathered against her, I will make Jerusalem an immovable rock for all the nations. All who try to move it will injure themselves......(9) On that day I will set out to destroy all the nations that attack Jerusalem.*
>
> **Mourning for the One They Pierced**
> *10 "And I will pour out on the house of David and the inhabitants of Jerusalem a spirit of grace and supplication.* ***They will look on me, the one they have pierced,*** *and they*

> *will mourn for him as one mourns for an only child, and grieve bitterly for him as one grieves for a firstborn son. 11 On that day the weeping in Jerusalem will be great, like the weeping of Hadad Rimmon in the plain of Megiddo.*
> (Zechariah 12:1-2,9-11 NIV)

As the Arabs attacked Israel on this Feast Day in 1973, the Antichrist will probably attack Israel around this time in some future year. This time Jesus will return to fight the final battle of Armageddon and Israel will mourn when they realize it was their Messiah that they killed.

<u>Feast of Trumpets</u>
Just prior to the Day of Atonement is the Feast of Trumpets also known as Rosh Hashanah. The Feast of Trumpets falls on the 1$^{st}$ and 2$^{nd}$ of Tishri and begins at the sighting of the new moon the evening before Tishri 1.

Most prophecy students believe that the Rapture of the Church will take place on this Feast day and many books have been written and the Internet is filled with information on why this is the most likely day for the Rapture of the Church. We also believe this will be the day for the Main Harvest Rapture of the Church that is Left Behind when God removes the wise virgins who were members of the church of Philadelphia in the Firstfruit Rapture on Pentecost. Here again please see our book: ***The Coming Spiritual Earthquake*** which is available as a PDF version for free by visiting our Website: www.ProphecyCountdown.com

Suffice it to say, we believe most of the Church will have to endure the Tribulation period before the Lord comes on the Feast of Trumpets to Rapture His Church. Had the foolish virgins been obedient to the Lord's command they may have been taken earlier:

> *"**Watch** ye therefore, and **pray always**, that ye **may be accounted worthy to escape** all these things that shall come to pass, and to stand before the Son of man."* (Luke 21:36)

Feast of Dedication

Hanukkah, also known as the Festival of Lights is the Feast of Dedication that falls between Kislev 24 to Kislev 31 (December). This Feast day lasts 8 days and was a celebration that Jesus observed (John 10:22-23).

It was a popular and joyous festival commemorating the purifying of the Temple, the removal of the old polluted altar, and the restoration of the worship of Jehovah. Jewish Tradition says that when the sacred "lamp stands" of the restored Temple were to be lighted there was only enough oil for one day but miraculously the oil remained filled for eight days. Hence this Feast is known as the Festival of Lights and it is celebrated over an 8 day period. The celebration was always of a joyous, exuberant character which commemorated the restoration of the worship of the Temple (1 Macc. 4:41-49). God also makes this promise through his prophet:

> *"Consider now from this day and upward, from the **four and twentieth day of the ninth** month, even from the day that the foundation of the LORD'S temple was laid, consider it.... (19)...from this day will I bless you. (23) In that day, saith the LORD of hosts, will I take thee... and will make thee as a signet: for I have chosen thee, saith the LORD of hosts."* (Haggai 2:18-19,23)

The future fulfillment of this day could be the grand celebration that takes place at the end of the Tribulation period as the Millennium is about to commence. In Chapter 4, we saw that Daniel 12:12 promises a **blessing** for those who reach the end of the 1,335 day period:

> *"**Blessed** is he that waiteth, and cometh to the thousand three hundred and five and thirty days."* (Daniel 12:12)

This is the last count of days found in the book of Daniel and it indicates that whoever reaches the end of this period will be blessed. Final realization that the Tribulation Period is over will be great reason for celebration, and the Feast of Dedication could be the Feast day we will be celebrating the start of the 1,000 rule and reign with our Lord and Saviour Jesus Christ. Very interestingly,

1335 days from the Feast of Dedication usually falls somewhere during the Feasts around Passover which leads us to the following:

Feast of Passover, Unleavened Bread and First Fruits
Passover followed by Unleavened Bread is celebrated for 8 days and begins on the 15$^{th}$ day of Nissan. Since the Jewish day begins at sun down, Passover actually starts at sundown on the 14$^{th}$.

Passover has four primary levels of significance: (1) Passover is an historical festival, commemorating the exodus from Egypt; (2) Passover is an agricultural festival, (3) Passover is a religious festival that celebrates the fact that God redeemed Israel and (4) Jesus fulfilled these Springtime Feasts by His death, burial and resurrection as pictured in the diagram found on the following page.

The future fulfillment of these Feasts are not known for 100% certainty, however, as was noted above in our discussion of the Feast of Dedication, backing up 1,335 days (Daniel 12:12) from the Feast of Dedication always brings us to the Springtime Feasts 3 years previously. This inter-connectivity between these appointed times must be by Divine design since Daniel was led by the Holy Spirit to write this important prophecy.

As discussed in Chapter 4, the 2 Witnesses will arrive on the world scene at some point near the very beginning of the Tribulation period. We know it must be near the start of this period because they are given 1,260 days or 3 ½ years to carry out their ministry. When their work is completed they will be killed by the Antichrist and their dead bodies will be allowed to lay in the streets of Jerusalem for 3 ½ days. After this they are Raptured into heaven and this point marks the end of the 2$^{nd}$ of 3 Woes with the 3$^{rd}$ Woe about to take place.

This must mean that the 2 Witnesses arrive somewhere near the very start of the tribulation period and places their arrival around the time of the Springtime Feasts. In the **Endtime Timelines** found at the back of this book, their arrival occurs sometime during these Springtime Feasts.

# Passover Fulfilled by Jesus

| Tuesday | Wednesday | Thursday | Friday | Saturday | Sunday |
|---------|-----------|----------|--------|----------|--------|
|         | Passover  | Unleavened Bread | | Weekly Sabbath | First Fruits |
| 04/08/32 | 04/09/32 | 04/10/32 | 04/11/32 | 04/12/32 | 04/13/32 |

* Last Supper (04/08/32)

04/09/32:
- Condemned → 9 am
- 3 pm ← Died
- Buried

04/12/32: Arose → *
* Ascended (04/13/32)

First Day Begin → * | Ends → *

Passover began on the evening of the previous day when Jesus had the Last Supper with His disciples. Unleavened Bread follows as a 7 day Feast and First Fruits always falls after the Weekly Sabbath (i.e. always on a Sunday)

## 10th OF AV

The final Feast Day we will look at in this Chapter known as the 10th of AV has played an important part in the history of the Jewish people and the world. In Grant Jeffrey's book: ***Armageddon*** he outlines eight very significant events that happened on this day:

1) Promised Land lost by Israel due to their rebellion and unbelief.
2) **Solomon's Temple destroyed – 587 BC**
3) **Second Temple destroyed – 70 AD**
4) Romans plowed Jerusalem – 71 AD
5) Bar Kochba's Army destroyed in 135 AD
6) England expelled Jews in 1290 AD
7) Spain expelled Jews in 1492 AD
8) World War I declared.

   **+ 2 more recent events:**
9) Israel gave back Gaza (God's land) 2005
10) Greatest number of deaths in Lebanon War 2006

Notice that both the 1st and 2nd Temples have been destroyed on this day: the 10th of AV!

Could it be that the Jewish religious leaders re-establish their Temple (see Chapter 8) to only have it destroyed again for the 3rd time on this Feast Day? Daniel 8:14's possible count of 1,150 days could begin on this Feast Day. In the past, terrible events have taken place on this day. Will history repeat itself once again?

## **COUNT OF DAYS**

As outlined in Chapter 4, Daniel and Revelation indicate three main counts of days: 1,260 days, 1,290 days and 1,335 days. In developing the **Endtime Timelines**, it was discovered that these time periods overlap one another in intriguing ways.

As shown in the following diagrams, God may have designed these prophetic days to overlap and find their fulfillment connected to the various Feast Days described earlier.

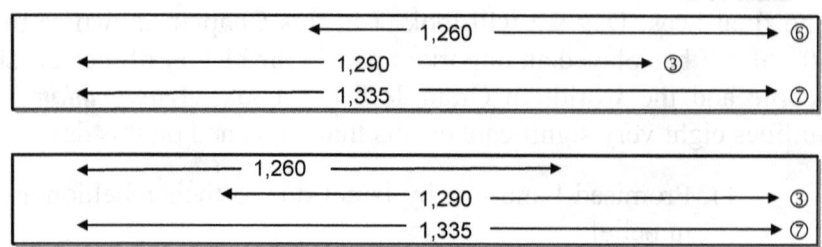

The fulfillment of Biblical Prophecy centers around the Feasts Days outlined in this Chapter. Paul said these were *"shadows of things to come"* (Colossians 2:16-17). Jesus said that the entire word of God must be fulfilled. These days overlap in such as way that there is either a 75 or 45 day period separating events on either side (beginning or ending) with a period of 1,215 days in the very middle. Only the divine hand of God could have orchestrated the sun, moon and the earth along with His inspired Word. Our God truly is an Awesome God!

Interestingly, it was discovered that there may actually be a "double' fulfillment of both sets of counts. The set of counts at the top[4] could be fulfilled at the very beginning of the Tribulation Period with the set of counts at the bottom being fulfilled at its very end.

In Chapter 8, we will look at some of the key events that could act as milestones in the Endtime events that will fulfill God's overall plan.

# Chapter 7 – Feast of Pentecost

As discussed in the last Chapter, the Feast of Pentecost is the most likely day for the Rapture of Firstfruit Believers. Firstfruit Believers are those Christians also characterized by the *"5 wise virgins"* who are found looking and ready when the Bridegroom returns. They are described in the book of Revelation as the Church of Philadelphia who are given the wonderful promise of escaping the Tribulation period:

> *"(8) I know thy works: behold, I have set before thee an open door, and no man can shut it: for thou hast a little strength, and hast **kept my word, and hast not denied my name**.... (10) **Because thou hast kept the word of my patience**, I also **will keep thee from the hour of temptation**, which shall come upon all the world, to try them that dwell upon the earth"* (Revelation 3:8 & 10)

The Firstfruit Believer is obedient to the word of God and found doing what the Word says to do and not merely listening to it:

> *"¶ (21) Wherefore lay apart all filthiness and superfluity of naughtiness, and receive with meekness the engrafted word, which is able to save your souls. (22) **But be ye doers of the word**, and **not hearers only**, deceiving your own selves."* (James 1:21-22)

Also, the Firstfruit Believers are those Christians who have demonstrated that they have died to their old life by allowing the Holy Spirit to control their lives so they become what the word of God describes as overcomers:

> *"(21) **To him that overcometh** will I grant to sit with me in my throne, even as I also overcame, and am set down with my Father in his throne. (22) He that hath an ear, let him hear what the Spirit saith unto the churches"*
> (Revelation 3:21-22)

The Firstfruit Believers are those wise and faithful Christians who are filled with the Holy Spirit (empowered and directed by) which enables them to be overcomers. As a result, these Christians will rule and reign with Christ when He returns. In our book: **The Coming Spiritual Earthquake** we go into greater detail and describe the requirements for being among the Firstfruit Believers and how to prepare to meet the Bridegroom.

Pentecost = Rapture Feast ?
The Holy Spirit came 50 days after the resurrection to empower and anoint Believers for the ministry of the Church. We believe the Lord could remove those anointed Firstfruit Believers who are *"filled with the Holy Spirit"* on this same Feast Day.

As we approach the time of the Rapture, it would be beneficial to remember the story of Noah. In this story, God told Noah the exact day of his deliverance 7 days in advance:

> *"Seven days from now I will send rain on the earth for forty days and forty nights, and I will wipe from the face of the earth every living creature I have made."*
> (Genesis 7:4 – NIV)

Jesus told us in Matthew 24:27: *"As it was in the days of Noah, so it will be at the coming of the Son of Man."* Remember from Chapter 2, the wise and faithful followers of Jesus are to know the time of their deliverance. As Noah knew the time of the Great Flood, we believe that we can and should know the time of the Lord's return. Since Jesus said His coming will be the same as it was as in Noah's day it would be advantageous to look into this time a little closer.

Remember, the days of Noah also include the time of Noah's great grandfather Enoch:

> *"Enoch walked with God; then he was no more because God took him away."* (Genesis 5:24)

Enoch was the first person to ever be Raptured from the earth. Because Enoch walked with God, God removed him from the earth

# Feast of Pentecost

prior to when the Great Flood arrived. While the word of God does not indicate when this event occurred, there is a book entitled: ***The Secrets of Enoch*** which records that Enoch was Raptured on his birthday, the sixth of Sivan. The sixth of Sivan just happens to be the Feast of Pentecost. Enoch was born and Raptured on the Feast of Pentecost!

Another name for **Pentecost** is the **Feast of Weeks** or the **Feast of Harvest**. Notice that there are three annual festivals:

> *"(14) ¶ Three times thou shalt keep a feast unto me in the year. (15) Thou shalt keep the feast of unleavened bread: (thou shalt eat unleavened bread seven days, as I commanded thee, in the time appointed of the month Abib; for in it thou camest out from Egypt: and none shall appear before me empty:)*
> *(16) And **the feast of harvest, the firstfruits of thy labours**, which thou hast sown in the field: and the feast of ingathering, which is in the end of the year, when thou hast gathered in thy labours out of the field."* (Exodus 23:14-16)

Notice that the 2$^{nd}$ of the three annual festivals is known as the Feast of Harvest and also know as the Feast of Weeks:

> *"(22) Celebrate the **Feast of Weeks** with the **firstfruits of the wheat harvest…"*** (Exodus 34:22 – NIV)

The Feast of Weeks was the harvest festival celebrated with the Firstfruits of the wheat harvest (Matthew 3:12 and 13:30). The **Feast of Weeks** or **Pentecost** is the time of celebration for the Firstfruits of the wheat crop. Pentecost is actually called the **day of Firstfruits:**

> *"On **the day of firstfruits**, when you present to the Lord an offering of new grain during the Feast of Weeks,…"*
> (Numbers 28:26 – NIV)

The day of Firstfruits is **Pentecost.** Enoch was Raptured on Pentecost as a type picture of the Firstfruit Believer. Because Enoch pleased God by walking with Him, God Raptured Enoch as a type picture on the day of Firstfruits or Pentecost.

Based upon this beautiful similitude, the Feast of Pentecost could very well be the time for God to Rapture His Firstfruit Believers from the earth. It is the day of Firstfruits and a Feast of Harvest. For those Firstfruit Believers walking with God, the Rapture could take them home to be with Him on this same day, the anniversary of the Rapture of Enoch, the day of Firstfruits.

Enoch was born and Raptured on his Birthday. Enoch is a type of Firstfruit Believer since he is described as one who **walked with** God and **he pleased** God. The Holy Spirit came 50 days after the resurrection to empower and **"anoint" Believers** for the ministry of the Church. On this same Feast Day, the Lord could remove those **"anointed" Firstfruit Believers** who are found pleasing in the sight of God because they are walking with God by being *"filled with the Holy Spirit."*

Since Enoch was born and Raptured on the **Feast of Pentecost**, and **Pentecost** is the actual **day of Firstfruits** in celebration of the harvest of the Firstfruits wheat crop, God could harvest His Firstfruit Believers on this day: the **Feast of Pentecost**. It would be prior to the general harvest at the Feast of Ingathering (Exodus 23:16) which will take place at the end of the Tribulation. God removes the Firstfruits in the Spring at Pentecost, followed by the Main Harvest after the hot summer sun in the Fall on the Feast of Trumpets. As God removed Enoch prior to the time of the Great Flood, God should also remove Enoch's protégés (the Firstfruit Believers) prior to the Great Tribulation.

---

The **Firstfruit Believer** is obedient to the word of God and is a member of the Church of Philadelphia. They are the *"5 Wise Virgins"* who have done what the word of God says to do and they are *"filled with the Spirit"* (Ephesians 5:18) which is evidenced by the **extra measure of oil** that they carried in their jars. They are actively waiting and watching for their Bridegroom to return for their wedding day praying:

***"Watch** ye therefore, and **pray always**, that ye **may be accounted worthy to escape** all these things that shall come to pass, and to stand before the Son of man."* (Luke 21:36)

# Chapter 8 – Possible Coming Events

FALSE PEACE ?

The popular "Traditional" teaching says that the Antichrist will come to confirm a 7 Year Treaty that he will break after 3 ½ years. We now know that this is a human tradition that is not what the Word of God says. While this teaching is false, there are certain elements that may prove to be partially correct.

The Middle East has been and will continue to be the key region where Endtime events will be carried out. Most of the Arab nations want to see Israel removed from their land and we know that the Bible predicts a time when Israel will be driven into the wilderness for a period of approximately 3½ years (see Chapter 4).

Before that occurs, the Word of God does indicate that a period of apparent peace will arrive:

> *"(1) But of the times and the seasons, brethren, ye have no need that I write unto you. (2) For yourselves know perfectly that the **day of the Lord** so cometh as a thief in the night. (3) **For when they shall say, Peace and safety;** then **sudden destruction cometh** upon them, as travail upon a woman with child; and they shall not escape.*
>
> *(4) But ye, brethren, are not in darkness, that that day should overtake you as a thief. (5) Ye are all the children of light, and the children of the day: we are not of the night, nor of darkness. (6) Therefore let us not sleep, as do others; but let us **watch and be sober**."* (I Thess. 5:1-6)

Paul tells us that *"**sudden destruction**"* is coming but just before it comes there will be an apparent time when everyone believes that *"**Peace and Safety**"* has finally arrived. This time will really be a **"FALSE PEACE"** since we know that the Bible says destruction will soon follow.

Christians should not be in darkness about these facts but should be watching and praying:

> *"Watch ye therefore, and **pray always**, that ye **may be accounted worthy to escape** all these things that shall come to pass, and to stand before the Son of man."* (Luke 21:36)

If Christians are not watching and praying this, the sudden destruction that is coming will surprise them – since a thief comes at a time when you are not expecting him.

The main point is that Israel may enter into a Peace accord with the Arabs and they may believe a time of peace and security has arrived. According to the Word of God, it will be a FALSE PEACE and sudden destruction will occur shortly thereafter.

TABERNACLE RECOVERED ?
The title of this Chapter is **"Possible Coming Events."** It is not known for 100% certainty, but it is possible that Israel may discover the location of the Tabernacle of David that was hidden by Jeremiah:

> *"**(4)** It was also contained in the same writing, that the prophet, being warned of God, commanded the tabernacle and the ark to go with him, as he went forth into the mountain, where Moses climbed up, and saw the heritage of God. (5) And when Jeremy came thither, he found an hollow cave, wherein he laid the tabernacle, and the ark, and the altar of incense, and so <u>stopped the door.</u> (6): And some of those that followed him came to mark the way, but they could not find it. (7) Which when Jeremy perceived, he blamed them, saying, As for that place, it shall be unknown until the time that God gather his people again together, and receive them unto mercy. (8) Then shall the Lord shew them these things, and the glory of the Lord shall appear, and the cloud also, as it was shewed under Moses, and as when Solomon desired that the place might be honourably sanctified."* (II Maccabees 2:4-8)

The Revised Standard Version of II Maccabees 2:4-8 reads:

> "**It was also in the writing that the prophet, having received an oracle, ordered that the tent and the ark should follow with him, and that he went out to the mountain where Moses had gone up and had seen the inheritance of God.** 5**And Jeremiah came and found a cave, and he brought there the tent and the ark and the altar of incense, and he <u>sealed up the entrance.</u>** 6Some of those who followed him came up to mark the way, but could not find it. 7When Jeremiah learned of it, he rebuked them and declared: "**The place shall be unknown until God gathers his people together again and shows his mercy.** 8**And then the Lord will disclose these things, and the glory of the Lord and the cloud will appear, as they were shown in the case of Moses, and as Solomon asked that the place should be specially consecrated.**"

While these writings are not included in the final Canon of the Bible, II Maccabees was one of the fourteen books of the Apocrypha which was taken out of modern translations in 1885 AD (after being part of Scriptures for around 2,000 years). According to the author, the tent, the ark and the altar of incense were hidden in a cave that was sealed up until the time that God gathers Israel back into the land.

The Tabernacle was a tent made out of fine linen and used by the Jewish people for worship services. Just before the Babylonian army siege of Jerusalem over 2,500 years ago it was hidden in a cave on Mount Nebo. The recovery of the hidden Tabernacle is also alluded to by the Prophet Amos:

> *"(11) ¶ In that day will I raise up the **tabernacle of David** that is fallen, and close up the breaches thereof; and I will raise up his ruins, and I will build it as in the days of old: (14) And I will bring again the captivity of my people of Israel, and they shall l build the waste cities, and inhabit them; and they shall plant vineyards, and drink the wine*

*thereof; they shall also make gardens, and eat the fruit of them. (15) And I will plant them upon their land, and they shall no more be pulled up out of their land which I have given them, saith the LORD thy God."*

(Amos 9:11,14-15)

God promises to return His people to the land He gave them. When the *"tabernacle of David"* will be recovered is not known, but it could be one of the signs that precedes or starts the final prophetic clock to start ticking again.

"Moses' Tabernacle in the Wilderness" was the dwelling place of God on the earth shown to Moses by a vision recorded in Exodus 25: 8-9; a pattern of the Holy places in Heaven according to Hebrews 9:23-24.

In his book, "Christ in the Tabernacle", A. B. Simpson said, "The Tabernacle is the grandest of all the Old Testament types of Christ. It was all one great object lesson of spiritual truth. In its wonderful furniture, priesthood, and worship, we see, with a vividness that we find nowhere else, the Glory and Grace of Jesus, and the privileges of His redeemed people".  Artist Norbert McNulty has faithfully researched the authenticity of this setting for his stunning painting. Hopefully it will inspire many more to search the scriptures. The above beautiful painting can be purchased from the following website: www.selahart.com

The first time David's Tabernacle was used was recorded in the book of I Chronicles:

> *"(1) ¶ So they brought the ark of God, and set it in the midst of the tent that David had pitched for it: and they offered burnt sacrifices and peace offerings before God. (2) And when David had made an end of offering the burnt offerings and the peace offerings, he blessed the people in the name of the LORD. (3) And he dealt to every one of Israel, both man and woman, to every one a loaf of bread, and a good piece of flesh, and a flagon [of wine]."*
> (I Chronicles 16:1-3)

Gary Stearman with ***Prophecy in the News*** [5] noted the following in his excellent article on the ***Tabernacle of David***:

"Scripture makes it clear that even David considered his tent only a temporary measure, pending the construction of a true Temple. Shortly after the Ark was inaugurated, he began to express his disappointment over the matter:

> *"(1) ¶ And it came to pass, when the king sat in his house, and the LORD had given him rest round about from all his enemies; (2) That the king said unto Nathan the prophet, See now, I dwell in an house of cedar, but the ark of God dwelleth within curtains"*. (II Samuel 7:1-2)

"The word of the Lord came to Nathan and David was told that his son would build the Temple. First there was to be a temporary tent, then a permanent building. Currently the thinking of the Sanhedrin reflects precisely this order of events – a temporary building of some sort, to be followed at the appropriate time by a permanent building. Currently, they plan a prefabricated structure. But if David's actual Tabernacle were found, they would quickly seize upon the opportunity to use it."

As Gary's article points out, if the Tabernacle of David is found, the Jewish religious leaders would be ecstatic and want to put it to immediate use. God's timing is perfect, and the recovery of David's Tabernacle could be one of the events to take place near the time when Daniel's **prophetic Clock** starts ticking again.

While studying Daniel 12:11 an interesting possible discovery was made. When looking into the actual meaning of the Hebrew[6] words we found something worth considering:

> *"(11) And from the time [that] the daily [sacrifice]* ***shall be taken away****, and the abomination that maketh desolate set up, there shall be a thousand two hundred and ninety days."* (Daniel 12:11)

[that] the daily [08548] [Note: words in brackets not in original text]
[sacrifice] **shall be taken away** [5493] where 5493 can mean**: to be removed**

The <u>first</u> use of this word in Scripture was very interesting:

> *(13) ¶ And it came to pass in the six hundredth and first year, in the first [month], the first [day] of the month, the waters were dried up from off the earth: and* ***Noah removed [5493] the covering of the ark****, and looked, and, behold, the face of the ground was dry."* (Genesis 8:13)

Noah **removed** the covering of the ark. Could Daniel 12:11 mean that someone will discover where David's Tabernacle and the Ark of the Covenant are located and **remove** the stones that are covering the cave where Jeremiah hid them?

The above discovery may mean absolutely nothing. However, it could mean that David's Tabernacle and the Ark are **removed** from that hidden cave on Mount Nebo and that event could start Daniel's **prophetic Clock** to start ticking.

MIDNIGHT CRY
As discussed in previous Chapters, the arrival of God's 2 witnesses will take place near the very beginning of the Tribulation Period.

Whether these witnesses are Enoch and Elijah or Moses and Elijah or someone else is not known for certainty. But we do know that they will arrive. Their appearance will be a most startling event for mankind. To the Jewish people it will be a wake-up call that their prophesied Messiah is about to return for the Second time. For the Arabs it will signal that their time is about up also.

For the Christians, it could be the announcement Jesus referred to in Matthew 25:

> *"(6) And **at midnight** there was **a cry made, Behold, the bridegroom cometh**; go ye out to meet him.*
> *(7) Then all those virgins arose, and trimmed their lamps.*
> *(8) And the foolish said unto the wise, Give us of your oil; for our lamps are gone out. (9) But the wise answered, saying, Not so; lest there be not enough for us and you: but go ye rather to them that sell, and buy for yourselves. (10) And while they went to buy, the **bridegroom came**; and **they that were ready** **went in with him to the marriage**: and the door was shut."* (Matthew 25:6-10)

Here we see that only the five wise virgins who were **READY** went into the wedding. The five foolish virgins were not properly prepared or ready when the Bridegroom arrived. This is a picture of the Church today. Many appear to be very busy, but they are not making the proper preparations. They are not busy making themselves ready to meet their Bridegroom. The Church needs to learn a lesson from the five wise virgins and prepare their lives to be ready to meet the Bridegroom: Jesus, when He returns for His Bride.

The appearance of the 2 Witnesses could be the **"cry made"** at **"midnight"** to the Church: **"Behold, the Bridegroom"** is coming! When the 2 Witnesses appear everyone will know that the Lord's return is at hand. The Wise Virgins who are ready will know that their time of deliverance has come! The Foolish Virgins, however, will realize that they have not been living for Jesus up until that time. At this point they will realize that they are not ready, but the parable indicates that the door will be shut and they will miss the Firstfruits Rapture! For more information on getting ready to make sure you are really ready, please see the free copy of the PDF version of our book: ***The Coming Spiritual Earthquake*** by going to: www.ProphecyCountdown.com

When the 2 Witnesses arrive very little time will remain. According to the calculations in our **Endtime Timelines**, only approximately 50 days may remain before Jesus calls His Firstfruit Believers home.

CLOCK TO START TICKING

We do not know what event will take place to start Daniel's **prophetic Clock** to begin ticking once again. It could be when Israel reaches a final peace accord with the Arabs and they believe that *"Peace and Safety"* has finally arrived. It also could be the discovery of David's Tabernacle from the cave in Mount Nebo, or it could possibly be the appearance of God's 2 Witnesses who arrive in Jerusalem to start their prophesying. Once it begins ticking again there will only be approximately 3 ½ years remaining until Jesus returns to set up His new Kingdom and where His faithful saints will be honored to rule and reign with Him.

Once the **prophetic Clock** starts ticking, there may be two additional mileposts known as the *"Abomination of Desolation."* It may be two, because their may be two different events that take place at different times. That is the subject of the next Chapter.

# Chapter 9 – Abomination of Desolation

## 2 SEPARATE ABOMINATIONS

The popular "Traditional" teaching about the *"Abomination of Desolation"* says that the Antichrist will arrive on the scene and confirm a 7 Year Peace Treaty, but after 3 ½ Years he will break the Treaty and then put an end to the Sacrifices that the Jewish people are making in their re-built Temple. This theory says that the Antichrist will enter the Temple of God <u>after</u> 3 ½ years declaring that he is God and do away with the animal Sacrifices. This is the traditional "Abomination" held by the vast majority of Believers alive today.

Again, while this teaching is false, there are certain elements about it that may prove to be partially correct. But first, let's look into what the definitions are from the two Gospels of Matthew and Luke.

> <u>Matthew 24</u>
> *"(15) ¶ When ye therefore shall see the **abomination of desolation**, spoken of by Daniel the prophet, **stand in the holy place**, (whoso readeth, let him understand:) (16) Then let **them** which be **in Judaea flee into the mountains**: (21) For then shall be **great tribulation**, such as was not since the beginning of the world to this time, no, nor ever shall be"* (Matthew 24:15-16,21).
>
> <u>Luke 21</u>
> *"(20) ¶ And when ye shall **see Jerusalem compassed with armies**, then know that **the desolation thereof is nigh**. (21) Then let **them** which are **in Judaea flee to the mountains**; and let them which are in the midst of it depart out; and let not them that are in the countries enter thereinto. (22) For these be the days of vengeance, that all things which are written may be fulfilled."* (Luke 21:20-22)

As can be seen by reading the two Gospels, there are actually two events in view. The first one in Matthew 24 occurs near the very start of the Tribulation period and the second one in Luke 21 occurs near the very end.

### 1st Abomination

In the Abomination of Desolation in Matthew 24, Jesus refers the reader to the Prophecy in the book of Daniel:

> Daniel 12
> *"(11) And from the time that the daily sacrifice shall be taken away, and the **abomination that maketh desolate set up**, there shall be a thousand two hundred and ninety days."* (Daniel 12:11)

Here Daniel indicates the abomination being set up in the holy place will begin the count of 1,290 days. Matthew says someone or something will be standing in the holy place. This could be fulfilled with the Antichrist arriving on the scene and entering the Temple the Jewish people have erected as was described in the previous Chapter. The religious leaders in Israel want to re-build the Temple and some form of sharing arrangement appears to be made that would allow them to do this. If this is the case, then the Abomination could be the Antichrist appearing at the Temple where he would declare that he is God. This was described by the Apostle Paul:

> *"(3) that **man of sin** be revealed, the son of perdition; (4) Who opposeth and **exalteth himself** above all that is called God, or that is worshipped; so that he as God **sitteth in the temple of God**, shewing himself that **he is God**."*
> (II Thessalonians 2:3-4)

If this interpretation is correct, then the Antichrist would arrive at the Temple and declare he is God. This event would start the clock ticking on the 1,290 days of Daniel 12:11.

But is this the only explanation? As was described in the previous Chapter, Daniel 12:11 could mean that someone will discover where David's Tabernacle and the Ark of the Covenant are located and **remove** the stones that are covering the cave where Jeremiah hid them. The actual discovery of David's Tabernacle and the Ark and their **removal** from that hidden cave on Mount Nebo could be the event that causes Daniel's **prophetic Clock** to start ticking.

A third possible explanation requires a little "thinking outside of the box" so to speak. The prophetic box created by human tradition can make us blind to what the Scriptures actually say.

Remember that we learned in Chapter 3, that Daniel 9:27 says, *"and in the midst of the week he shall cause the sacrifice and oblation to cease..."* After 3 ½ years of ministry, Jesus death on the cross forever ended God's requirement for man to offer animal sacrifices as atonement for sin. Jesus death on the cross literally caused the *"sacrifice and the oblation to cease"* forever more.

Daniel's **prophetic Clock** immediately stopped ticking when Jesus died on the cross. In God's eyes there will never be any need for animal sacrifices again. Daniel's final week or final 7 year period began when Jesus was baptized. His ministry lasted for a period of approximately 3 ½ years or in the "midst of the week." Daniel's **Clock** has stopped half way through the final week. Once the Clock starts ticking again there only remain approximately 3 ½ years:

**Daniel's Clock**
**Starts Ticking**

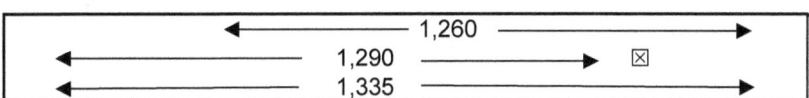

Under this Scenario, the Clock would start ticking by some event as described in the previous Chapter and then the Abomination would take place 1,290 days later where marked by the ☒ This view is completely different from our Traditional way of looking at things, but it could prove to be the correct view. But for now, let's look at the 2nd Abomination.

## 2nd Abomination

The Abomination described in Luke 21 is completely different from Matthew's description:

> *"(20) ¶ And when ye shall **see Jerusalem compassed with armies**, then know that **the desolation thereof is nigh**. (21) Then let **them** which are **in Judaea flee to the mountains…"** (Luke 21:20-21)*

Here Luke sees Jerusalem surrounded by armies[7] and he warns everyone to flee into the mountains. This is a picture of that future battle of Armageddon when all the Nations come against Israel to attempt to annihilate her. The Antichrist will lead the battle and it could be at this point that he sets up his command post in Jerusalem after the 2 Witnesses have been killed. The Antichrist could arrive at the Temple and declare he is God (II Thessalonians 2:3-4) before he is ultimately defeated by the King of Kings.

As can be seem from the above analysis, the correct solution to *"rightly divide the word"* is not easy. Our God is an Awesome God, and when He had men record His Words they were inspired by the Holy Spirit and we are reminded by the Prophet Isaiah: *"(8) For my thoughts are not your thoughts, neither are your ways my ways, saith the LORD."* (Isaiah 55:8)

God's wonderful Word sometimes has two or three fulfillments. God's way of thinking is so far above our ways and our thoughts. That is why we need to approach it with humility asking the Holy Spirit to teach us and to guide us. Hopefully the above analysis of the Abominations that are scheduled to take place will stir us to appreciate His Word even more.

## Animal Sacrifices

One final thought regarding the Abomination refers to the idea that the Jewish religious leaders want to rebuild the Temple in order to resume animal sacrifices. As we saw in Chapter 3, Jesus Christ performed the ultimate Sacrifice by dying for all mankind. If the Jewish people re-institute animal sacrifices, won't that be an ***"Abomination"*** in the sight of God?

Whether or not animal sacrifices are resumed, if they do, they certainly would not be acceptable to God. Jesus forever ended the need to sacrifice the blood of animals. His precious blood was poured out for our sins. Animal sacrifices could be the abomination that we have been discussing.

# Chapter 10 – Endtime Timeline

We are now ready to see how the information presented in the preceding chapters comes together in our **Endtime Timelines**. We need to begin by restating the fact that the purpose of these **Endtime Timelines** in not to set an EXACT date for any event. However, once these Endtime events are set in motion, the final count of days have been given to us in both the books of Daniel and Revelation. We also need to remember that we **are living** in the *"time of the end"* and that the prophecies in Daniel are to be *"unsealed"* at that time and that the *"wise will understand."*

Let's remember that Daniel's **prophetic Clock** stopped ticking when Jesus died on the cross:

> *"And he shall confirm the covenant with many **for one week: and in the midst of the week he shall cause the sacrifice and the oblation to cease**,* (Daniel 9:27)

Daniel's final week or final 7 year period began when Jesus was baptized. His ministry lasted for a period of approximately 3 ½ years or in the *"midst of the week."* Daniel's **prophetic Clock** was stopped half way through the final week.

We know that at some future point the clock is going to start ticking once again. In Chapter 5 we reviewed three possible times that Daniel's **prophetic Clock** could start. Daniel's last 3 ½ year period could begin:

|  |  |
|---|---|
| Scenario ① | January 1, 2009 |
| Scenario ② | March 17, 2009 |
| Scenario ③ | May 31, 2009 |

The calculations for these possible times are shown in Chart # 1 found at the end of the book.

Endtime Timeline: 2009-2012
The **Endtime Timeline** from 2009 to 2012 can be found in Chart # 2. It is worth commenting that this Chart # 2, was actually

developed approximately one month prior to the time Chart # 1 was prepared. In other words, the starting point for the **Endtime Timeline** was developed independently and prior to when the calculations were made for Chart # 1.

After all of the **Endtime Timelines** were developed, the question concerning the Length of the Generation that will witness the Return of the Messiah was addressed. The starting dates of March $17^{th}$ and May $31^{st}$ in 2009 that are shown on the **Endtime Timeline (Chart # 2)** were actual calculations that incorporated Daniel's count of days (1,260, 1,290 and 1,335) in relationship to God's Feast Days. Coincidentally, these same starting points on Chart # 2 were the exact same days that were arrived at in Chart # 1, where we show the calculations for the length of the generations!

Whether or not this is just a coincidence or confirmation that this **Endtime Timeline for 2009 to 2012** is correct is not known. We hope that it is confirmation that it is correct, but it could be merely a coincidence.

Does this mean that the Tribulation Period will begin in 2009? It does appear that things line up for Endtime events to begin in 2009. Could they begin in 2008? Yes, the Endtime events could begin in 2008, or they could begin after 2009. These **Endtime Timelines** may or may not prove to be accurate. As stated earlier in this book:

> *"For now we see through a glass, darkly; but then face to face: now I know in part; but then shall I know even as also I am known."* (I Corinthians 13:12)

The lens through which we view the Scriptures is not perfect. Through much prayer and fasting I have sincerely asked the Holy Sprit to guide me and to show me the truth that is hidden in the Word. I know that the Lord is coming very soon and most of the Church is completely unprepared for what lies ahead. My purpose in all of this has been to stir up those who are **"lukewarm"** so they can begin to prepare for what's coming. The mentality that has been created by the popular *Left Behind* phenomena leaves most in the Church thinking they all will be Raptured because they are Christians and they don't need to concern themselves with how they live their life. They have been told that Jesus will Rapture them to Heaven and they don't need to worry about all of this.

But if the discoveries made in this book are correct, then Endtime events are going to take place differently from what they have come to believe. It is time for the Church to Wake-up now while there is still time! Once the *"Midnight Cry"* goes out, it will be too late for the Foolish Virgins. There will not be enough time for them to prepare then and they will literally be left behind when Jesus comes for His Firstfruit Believers!

The **Endtime Timeline: 2009 to 2012** could prove to be correct. It represents the $42^{nd}$ Generation since Israel recovered the Old City of Jerusalem from the Gentiles in 1967. That event on June 7, 1967 was a major Prophetic Milestone and 2009 will be 42 years afterwards. As was discussed in Chapter 5, 42 is a significant number in relationship to both Israel and the $2^{nd}$ Coming of Jesus Christ.

Additional Corroboration?
There are also some additional interesting events that could take place in 2012, that would corroborate the **Endtime Timeline** for 2009 to 2012.

> *"(25) ¶ And there shall **be signs in the sun, and in the moon, and in the stars**; and upon the earth distress of nations, with perplexity; the sea and the waves roaring; (26) Men's hearts failing them for fear, and for looking after those things which are coming on the earth: **for the powers of heaven shall be shaken**"* (Matthew 25:25-26)

Signs in the Heavens
In the news in 2006 was the fact that scientists have discovered new information on the cycle of Sun Spot activity. According to their historical study, they have determined that the earth is going to enter into a period of intense sun spot activity beginning

sometime in 2008, with peak activity to arrive by the year 2012. If the **Endtime Timeline: 2009 to 2012** is correct, it could be validated by events that the scientists are predicting:

***Unprecedented Solar Storms Forecast*** (AP & UPI wires – 3/6/06)
"An intensification of storms on the surface of the sun in coming years could disrupt satellites, communications and power grids on earth and endanger astronauts. A new 11year cycle beginning in late 2007 or early 2008 will be up to 50% stronger than previous ones...**to reach their peak in 2012**." Forecasters say the solar storms "**can slow satellite orbits**" and are caused by twisted magnetic fields in the sun that suddenly snap and release tremendous amounts of energy."

Could satellites falling from the sky be what John saw in Revelation 6:13 at the 6th Seal?: *"the stars of heaven fell unto the earth, even as a fig tree casteth her untimely figs, when she is shaken of a mighty wind."* The scientists are predicting strong "solar winds" that could disrupt the orbits of the satellites. Are these the winds God will use to make the "stars" fall to the earth? The timing appears to coincide with the findings in the **Endtime Timeline** for 2009 to 2012.

Planet X
In recent years there has been much speculation about a possible 10th planet that was supposedly discovered by NASA back in the 1980's. While this is believed to be a major hoax perpetuated over the Internet, we do know that the book of Revelation tells us that a major celestial body will fall to the earth sometime toward the end of the Great Tribulation Period:

> *"(10) ¶ And the third angel sounded, and there fell a **great star from heaven**, burning as it were a lamp, and it fell upon the third part of the rivers, and upon the fountains of waters; (11) And the name of the star is called Wormwood: and the third part of the waters became wormwood; and many men died of the waters, because they were made bitter."* (Revelation 8:10-11)

John saw some large object from space falling to the earth. Whether this was a fragment of some comet, planet or asteroid is speculation but we do know that some celestial body will be responsible for this cataclysmic event that John saw.

Interestingly, there are some who are predicting Planet X could possibly affect planet Earth in 2012.[8] This may sound ridiculous and outrageous, but we do know that the prophecies in Revelation will take place sometime. When or how they will be fulfilled is open for speculation but we do know that they will take place. It is just a matter of when.

Other Possibilities

While the **Endtime Timeline** for 2009 to 2012, could prove to be correct, there are other possibilities. God's ways are higher than our ways and it is very difficult to know for certain when particular prophecies will occur. Once a prophecy is fulfilled, we can then point to where it was predicted in God's wonderful Word. Since we do not know for certain, Jesus instructed us as follow:

> *"And take heed to yourselves, lest at any time your hearts be overcharged with surfeiting and drunkenness, and cares of this life, and so that day come upon you unawares. For as a snare shall it come on all them that dwell on the face of the whole earth.* ***Watch*** *ye therefore, and* ***pray always****, that ye* ***may be accounted worthy to escape*** *all these things that shall come to pass, and to stand before the Son of man."* (Luke 21:34-36)

In the next Chapter, we will look a little deeper into Daniel's prophecy to see if there may be other possibilities.

# Chapter 11 – End of 7 Weeks?

In Chapter 3, we focused on the last verse in Daniel 9:

> *"(24) Seventy weeks are determined upon thy people and upon thy holy city, to finish the transgression, and to make an end of sins, and to make reconciliation for iniquity, and to bring in everlasting righteousness, and to seal up the vision and prophecy, and to anoint the most Holy."* **(25) Know therefore and understand, that from the going forth of the commandment to restore and to build Jerusalem unto the Messiah the Prince shall be seven weeks,** *and threescore and two weeks: the street shall be built again, and the wall, even in troublous times. (26) And after threescore and two weeks shall Messiah be cut off, but not for himself: and the people of the prince that shall come shall destroy the city and the sanctuary; and the end thereof shall be with a flood, and unto the end of the war desolations are determined. (27) And he shall confirm the covenant with many for one week: and in the midst of the week he shall cause the sacrifice and the oblation to cease, and for the overspreading of abominations he shall make it desolate, even until the consummation, and that determined shall be poured upon the desolate."* (Daniel 9:24-27)

Verse 27 has been the primary focus of this book so far because it is the one key verse that has been so terribly distorted and caused so much misinformation.

Before we shift our focus to Verse 25, it is important to point out that Daniel speaks of 70 weeks where one week is the equivalent of 7 years of time. So when Daniel says 70 weeks he is referring to 490 years. When he says 62 weeks he is talking about 434 years and when he says 7 weeks he is referring to 49 years. As was discussed earlier in this book, the 1 week period of time refers to 7 years where the first half or 3 ½ years was fulfilled by the ministry of Jesus from 28 AD to 32 AD and the second half of that week or 3 ½ years remains to be fulfilled during the Tribulation period.

Daniel 9:24, therefore is saying there will be 490 years at which time reconciliation for mankind's sins will be accomplished. In other words after this 490 year period, Jesus will have been crucified for the sins of the world. This 490 year period was fulfilled by Jesus from 4257 BC when the Jews returned to Jerusalem until Christ was killed on April 9$^{th}$ 32 AD (see Appendix B for Sir Isaac Newton's analysis of Daniel's prophecy).

Daniel then mentions a period of 7 weeks (49 years) and 62 weeks (434 years). Notice that Daniel does not say 62 and 7 weeks but says 7 weeks and 62 weeks. Most have miss-interpreted this to mean 69 weeks, as Newton points out in his analysis:

> "Thus have we in this short Prophecy, a prediction of all the main periods relating to the coming of the *Messiah*; **the time of his birth, that of his death, that of the rejection of the *Jews*, the** duration of the *Jewish* war whereby he caused **the city and sanctuary to be destroyed,** and the **time of his second coming...** <u>**We avoid also the doing violence to the language of *Daniel***</u>, by taking the *seven weeks* and *sixty two weeks* for one number. Had that been *Daniel*'s meaning, he would have said *sixty and nine weeks*, **and not** <u>*seven weeks*</u> and <u>*sixty two weeks*</u>, **a way of numbering used by no nation.**"

So we can see that Daniel did not say 69 weeks. He mentions 7 weeks or 49 years and 62 weeks or 434 years. Verse 26 says that **after** the 62 weeks the Messiah will be cut off. The birth of Jesus actually occurred 434 years after 4278 BC which fulfilled this 62 weeks since Jesus was cut off **after** this time. (4278 BC to 3 BC = 434 Years (62 x7). For an additional discussion, see Appendix B.

Now let's shift our focus back to Verse 25:

> *"(25) Know therefore and understand, that from the going forth of the commandment to restore and to build Jerusalem unto the Messiah the Prince shall be seven weeks..."*

# End of 7 Weeks?

To understand Daniel 9:25 better, it would be helpful to look at the words used in the original Hebrew:

> *"(25) Know therefore and understand, that from the going forth [4161] of the commandment [1697] to restore [7725] and to build [1129] Jerusalem unto the Messiah the Prince shall be seven weeks,"* (Daniel 9:25)

Where [4161] can mean: **bud** or **issue**
And [1697] can be interpreted to be: **report**
And [7725] can be interpreted to be: **recover**

A paraphrase of Daniel 9:25 might read:

> *"Know therefore and understand this: from the **issuing**(bud) of the **report** of **recovering** to rebuild **Jerusalem** until the time that the Messiah comes as Prince (or King) shall be 49 years"*

In other words, Daniel may be telling us that Jesus will come as King 49 years after the report of the recovery of Jerusalem takes place! When did the report of the recovery of Jerusalem take place? On June 7, 1967 when Israel recaptured the Old City of Jerusalem!

If this interpretation is correct, it is telling us the actual year Jesus will return as the Messiah the Prince or as King!

## 5776 – 49th YEAR

The report of the recovery of Jerusalem took place on June 7, 1967. This Prophetic Milestone took place during the Hebrew year 5727. The 49th year should end in 5776 on the Feast of Atonement: September 23, 2015. (5727 + 49 = 5776 where 5776 begins on the Feast of Trumpets: September 14, 2015)

If this interpretation of Daniel 9:25, is correct, it is telling us that Jesus will come as King at the Battle of Armageddon to defeat the Antichrist and the armies that will come against Israel.

According to Daniel, from the time of the report of the recovery of Jerusalem until Jesus comes to rule as King there will be 49 years. The **Endtime Timeline for 2012 to 2015** (Chart # 3) shows that Jesus may return in the Fall of 2015. This may be the correct final timeline if this interpretation of Daniel is accurate.

Sir Isaac Newton ended his commentary on this part of Daniel's prophecy by stating: ***"Let time be the Interpreter."*** Newton wrote on Daniel sometime before his death in 1733. If he were alive today, however, my guess is that Newton would understand that the prophecy concerning the 7 weeks relates to the 49 years that will culminate with the return of Jesus as King. Newton would probably be shouting from the rooftops, "Get Ready, Jesus is Coming!"

REVIEW OF FULFILLMENTS

As stated earlier in this book, our God is an awesome God! His Word is rich and wonderful and His ways are so much Higher than our ways and our way of thinking. In many passages throughout His Word, God has multiple fulfillments of prophecies. The prophecies of Daniel are no exception. Let's take a closer look at the last several verses of Daniel 9. The summary that can be viewed on the following page can help us understand how truly remarkable our God is. Take a moment to study this remarkable prophecy with your Bible open.

This summary shows that 4 prophecies have been fulfilled and 3 prophecies may remain to be fulfilled when Jesus returns. Now that we understand that this prophecy is not about the Antichrist, we can comprehend what remains to be fulfilled by our Messiah Jesus Christ!

The primary prophecy that we have brought into focus in this Chapter is # 3 on the summary found on Page 93. If the interpretation described earlier in this section is correct regarding Verse 25, then Daniel's prophecy does tell us the time of the $2^{nd}$ Coming (see Newton's comments about this in Appendix B).

## Review of Daniel 9:24-27

| # | Fulfillments | Weeks | Daniel 9 | Status |
|---|---|---|---|---|
| 1 | Christ Completes Reconciliation of Sin | 70 | Verse 24 | C |
| 2 | Christ's 1st Coming – Jesus Cut Off After | 62 | Verse 26 | C |
| 3 | Christ's 2nd Coming – **Jesus Comes as King** | 7 | **Verse 25** | R |
| 4 | Jesus Crucified (Sacrifices Cease) – End of | .5 | Verse 27 (1st Half) | C |
| 5 | Jesus Returns – End of Tribulation – End of | .5 / 70 | Verse 27 (2nd Half) | R |
| 6 | Jerusalem Desolation by Romans – End of | .5 | Verse 26 & 27 | C |
| 7 | Jerusalem Desolation 11H$^9$ at Armageddon – End of .5 | | Verse 26 & 27 | R |

**Status:** C – Completed or R – Remaining

This triggers the question, if Jesus will return for the Battle of Armageddon in the Fall of 2015, how do you explain that earlier Chapters show Daniel's **Prophecy Clock** could start Ticking again at the beginning of 2009? If there is only 3 ½ years remaining in Daniel's prophecy, how do you account for this?

Let's review what the 2 **Endtime Timelines** are saying:

|  | <u>Chart #2</u> | <u>Chart # 3</u> |
|---|---|---|
| Daniel's **Prophecy Clock** Begins Again | 3/17/2009 | 3/12/2012 |
| Tribulation Period | 3 ½ Years | 3 ½ Years |
| Battle of Armageddon | 9/26/2012 | 9/23/2015 |

It appears that both Charts # 2 and # 3 can't both be correct. Either one may be correct, but they both can not be correct unless we have overlooked something. Unless, elements of both Charts have truth that are somehow connected. While praying and fasting over this apparent paradox, the Lord revealed how the two Timelines are possibly connected.

<u>Endtime Timeline: 2009-2015</u>
It is possible that certain elements of both Charts # 2 and # 3 are true. By combining these elements, we may arrive at a possible solution.

The starting point for this Timeline could possibly be the Firstfruits Rapture in 2009. As was outlined in Chart # 2, the most likely time for this event is Pentecost which falls on May 31, 2009.

This would fulfill the information outlined in Chart # 1 that shows Jesus should come after 42 years (Length of Generation). If this is the case, then the Firstfruits Rapture could take place at this time, however, Daniel's clock may not start-up right away. There could be a delay before Daniel's **Prophetic Clock** begins ticking again. As shown in Chart # 4, Daniel's clock may not start until the Spring of 2012 as previously outlined in Chart # 3. In other words, Jesus would come for His Firstfruit Believers around Pentecost in 2009, but Daniel's **Prophetic Clock** would not immediately start. Daniel's prophecies would then begin in the Spring of 2012, and

# End of 7 Weeks?

Jesus would return for the battle of Armageddon on September 23, 2015.

Possible Confirmation

While developing the **Endtime Timeline** for the period from 2009 to 2015, it was discovered that there is a possible connection between the first two timelines.

> *13 ¶ Then I heard one saint speaking, and another saint said unto that certain [saint] which spake,* **How long shall be the vision concerning the daily sacrifice, and the transgression of desolation,** *to give both the sanctuary and the host to be* **trodden under foot?** *14 And he said unto me,* **Unto two thousand and three hundred days**; *then shall the sanctuary be cleansed."* (Daniel 8:13-14)

While the New International Version as well as several other versions note that this period of time is 2,300 evenings and morning where it could mean 1,150 actual days (that is 2,300 / 2 = 1,150) the King James version of 2,300 days could be correct.

If this period in Daniel 8 represents 2,300 days, then this could provide the resolution. If we start at May 31, 2009 and go forward 2,300 days we arrive at September 17, 2015. Now if we adjust the arrival of the Two Witnesses two days earlier than shown in Chart #3, they could arrive on the scene on April 6, 2012. Moving forward from here 1,260 days of their ministry takes us to September 17, 2015, the same day arrived at by adding the 2,300 days to Pentecost 2009!

The 2,300 days from Daniel 8:13-14, could provide the key that gives us the correct final Timeline. Since Daniel 8 is referring to the Sanctuary and the daily sacrifices, some Prophetic Milestone may take place on the Feast of Pentecost that would start this 2,300 day period to begin its final count. What that event might be is unknown, but it could be somehow related to the recovery of David's Tabernacle or the possible beginning of animal sacrifices at this time. This would mean that some unknown event would take place on May 31, 2009 that would end 2,300 days later on September 17, 2015. At that time the Sanctuary will be cleansed:

> *14 And he said unto me,* **Unto two thousand and three hundred days;** *then shall the sanctuary be cleansed [6663]."* (Daniel 8:14)
>
> Where [6663] can mean **made right** or **justified** or **vindicated**

At the end of the 2,300 days man's dominion over the Temple mount will be over. The 2 Witnesses will cease their ministry and their 1,260 days of Testimony for God will be over. The Sanctuary will now be made right and God will vindicate the ungodly by stepping onto the stage. Three and one-half days after the 2 Witnesses are killed, God will Rapture them to Heaven for all the world to see. Right after this Jesus Christ will return as the King of Kings to fight the final Battle of Armageddon. The end of the 2,300 days will mark the time when God will intervene to see that conditions are made right.

Other Possibilities
In Chapter 6, we discussed the fact there were 5 years for the periods examined from 2007 to 2017 that showed a correlation between the Feast of Pentecost and the Fall Feasts of either Atonement or Tabernacles.

Charts # 3 and # 4 extend out to 2015 as the end of the Tribulation Period and the only period beyond this time that was not included in this study was for the period from 2014 to 2017.

While **Endtime Timelines** could be developed for each of the years, we have decided to include only two additional timelines: Charts # 5 and # 6.

Chart # 5 – Timeline for 2008 to 2011
Chart # 5 is included because it assumes the $42^{nd}$ Year begins one year earlier than what was shown in Chart # 2. Very interestingly,

June 7, 2008 will be the 42$^{nd}$ birthday from the time the Old City of Jerusalem was recovered. Pentecost in 2008 falls on June 15$^{th}$ 2008, eight days after the generation turns 42. As was discussed in Chapter 5, the number 42 is a highly significant number relating to the timing for the return of the Lord. Chart # 5 could be the correct Endtime Timeline and Jesus could return for His faithful in 2008.

Chart # 6 – Timeline for 2014 to 2017
Chart # 6 is also included because it assumes the Second Coming could occur 50 years after the recovery of Jerusalem. Fifty is the year of Jubilee, so Chart # 6 could be the correct interpretation. Appendix E is provided for those Watchmen who may want to develop any additional Timelines not covered by this study.

Let Time Be The Interpreter

At this point it would be wise to heed the advice Sir Isaac Newton gave regarding Daniel 9:25. Even though we believe we may have an enlightened understanding of how these prophecies may be fulfilled, only time will reveal which of these final **Endtime Timelines** is correct.

As Newton said, "Let Time be the Interpreter."

The purpose of this study has been to alert the Church to the fact that Jesus is returning very soon and the Endtime events that will soon unfold could be entirely different from what everyone has been taught. Now, more that every before, all Christians need to be making preparations for the days ahead. Everyone needs to be entirely sure they are really ready.

Since we don't know the exact time for certain, we always need to be *"Watching"* and *"Praying"* as Jesus instructed us in order to be prepared and ready when He returns to take us home to be with Him (Luke 21:34-36).

# Chapter 12 – Preparation For Days Ahead

The Church is at the closing stages of this current dispensation and Jesus Christ is getting ready to return for His faithful Bride. Many in the Church have been unfaithful and not been obedient to the Lord and His Word. The Lukewarm Believers are in for a big surprise when Jesus comes to take His wise followers home.

This study of the prophecies in Daniel and Revelation should awaken those foolish virgins who have been lulled to sleep by the **Left Behind** mindset which tells them Jesus is coming to Rapture all Believers and you don't need to be concerned. The time of the end is at hand and Jesus is returning for those who are *"looking for Him"* and those who are *"filled with the Spirit."* Those Believers who have not been obedient and allowed their carnal nature to rule their lives will be left behind when Jesus comes for His devoted Bride. Have you responded to His Wedding Invitation?

<u>A Wedding Invitation</u>
The Great God of Heaven has announced in His Holy Word that a grand wedding is about to take place. Mankind's time on this earth is about up, and the Bridegroom is getting ready to return for His Bride. Are you part of the Bride of Christ? Will you be ready when Jesus returns?

Who is it that is invited to the wedding banquet? It is those described in Revelation 19:7 & 9:

> *"...For the wedding of the Lamb has come, and his bride has made herself ready...Then the angel said to me, "Write: Blessed are those who are invited to the wedding supper of the Lamb!"* And he added *"These are the true words of God."*

Notice that the above verse says, *"The bride made herself ready..."* How did she make herself ready?

> *"Fine linen, bright and clean, was given her to wear. (Fine linen stands for the **righteous acts** of the saints)"*
> (Revelation 19:8)

The Bride made herself ready for the wedding by obtaining her fine linen. This was her reward for her righteous deeds after she was saved. The original Greek confirms that this fine linen is not the righteousness that is imputed to every believer in Christ, but represents the **righteous acts** or the **righteous living** of the believer following their salvation. This same teaching was confirmed for us by Jesus when He taught about the ten virgins:

> *"At that time the kingdom of heaven will be like ten virgins who took their lamps and went out to meet the bridegroom. (v.2) Five of them were foolish and five were wise. (v.3) The foolish ones took their lamps but did not take any oil with them. (v.4) The wise, however, took oil in jars along with their lamps. (v.5) The bridegroom was a long time in coming, and they all became drowsy and fell asleep*[10].
>
> *(v.6) "At midnight the cry rang out: 'Here's the bridegroom! Come out to meet him!' (v.7) "Then all the virgins woke up and trimmed their lamps. (v.8) The foolish ones said to the wise, 'Give us some of your oil; our lamps are going out.' (v.9) "'No,' they replied, 'there may not be enough for both us and you. Instead, go to those who sell oil and buy some for yourselves' (v.10) "But while they were on their way to buy the oil, the bridegroom arrived. The **virgins who were ready** went in with him to the wedding banquet. And the door was shut."* (Matt. 25:4-10)

Here we see that only the five wise virgins who were ready went into the wedding. All 10 virgins were Christians because all did possess their oil which represents the Holy Spirit who was given to each of them upon their conversion. The 5 foolish virgins, however, did not carry along the extra measure of oil that the 5 wise virgins carried in their jars. The 5 wise virgins were ready because they were obedient to the Word of God which commands us to be *"filled with the Spirit"* (Ephesians 5:18). Because the 5 wise virgins were filled with the Spirit, they allowed Him to direct and empower their life. As a result, they were ready when the Bridegroom came at the midnight hour. Are you a wise or foolish

## Preparation For Days Ahead

virgin today? If the Bridegroom came today, would you be ready to go into the wedding? Will you accept the invitation? Why not make the following prayer the prayer of your heart right now:

> *"Dear God in Heaven, I realize that I have not been living my life for you. I humbly turn to you right now and ask you to forgive me. Dear Jesus, please rule and reign in my heart and life. Please help me to live for you for whatever time remains. I pray that I may be able to escape all that is about to happen, and that I may be able to stand before you when you return for me. In Jesus' name I pray. Amen"*

Our prayer is that many in the Church will pray this prayer and ask the Lord to help them be prepared for the days ahead. We do not know for certain when Jesus will return and which, if any, of the **Endtime Timelines** may be correct.

We really need to be ready and watching every day because we do not know for sure. We are also praying that this study will provoke you to examine the Scriptures on your own and motivate you to search out all the Holy Spirit wants to show you in the wonderful Bible. There is an old acronym that may seem corny, but it's true:

> B – Basis
> I – Instruction
> B – Before
> L – Leaving
> E – Earth

All Christians would do well to pay attention to this simple acronym because all Believers will be required to appear before the Judgement Seat of Christ. The Bible has all the answers Christians need. Let's look at what lies ahead for every Believer:

> *(9) Wherefore we labour, that, whether present or absent, we may be accepted of him. (10) For* ***we must all appear before the judgment seat of Christ****; that every one may receive the things done in his body, according to that he hath done, whether it be good or bad.* (II Corin. 5:9-10)

## JUDGEMENT SEAT OF CHRIST

As we approach the time of the Rapture, we would be remiss if we did not mention what lies ahead after we are taken to be with the Lord. Notice that the above Scripture says we will all appear before the Judgement Seat of Christ. This is a Judgement Seat before our Lord to give an account for our lives and all that we have done, whether good or bad.

### Shock And Surprise
While we long to be with our precious Lord and Saviour, we wonder how many are really ready to face the Judgement Seat of Christ? We even ask ourselves, are we really ready to meet Jesus?

After the Rapture takes place, many Christians will experience a great deal of shock and surprise. The Lukewarm believers will be left on the earth to face their time of testing under the Antichrist; while the faithful, wise believers will be taken to be with the Lord forever!

What is it that distinguishes between these two groups? Why were some wise and why were some foolish? Why were some ready, while others taken by surprise like a thief?

### Doctrine of Rewards
One of the biggest failures of the modern day Church has been not teaching on rewards. Most Christians believe they automatically will receive rewards due to the fact they have been saved. They have not been properly taught what the Word of God actually says:

***Salvation is by grace, but rewards are given according to works!***

> *"And, behold, I come quickly; and my reward is with me, to give every man according as his **work** shall be"*(Rev.22:12)

Most Christians know and can even quote Ephesians 2:8-9:
> *"For by grace are ye saved through faith; and that not of yourselves: it is the gift of God: Not of works, lest any man should boast."* (Ephesians 2:8-9)

But how many Christians realize the verse that follows:

> *"For we are God's workmanship, created in Christ Jesus **to do good works**, which God prepared in advance for us to do."* (Ephesians 2:10 – NIV)

While we are saved by Grace, we were saved to do the good Works that God actually created us to do! By focusing on Grace, the Church has not been taught how important Works are in the sight of God.

The Book of Revelation mentions Works nineteen times. Nineteen is the combination of 10 (Divine Order) and 9 (Judgement), which indicates that Works are symbolic of the Divine Order related to the Judgement of God.

> *"Knowing therefore the terror of the Lord, we persuade men..."* (II Corinthians 5:11)

The Church loves to hear sermons on the Love of God, but few pastors and teachers are brave enough to talk about the *"terror of the Lord."* The Judgement Seat of Christ will not be a pleasant experience for those Christians who have been living unfaithful lives. All deeds, true motives and designs will be laid bare before the Lord. The Christian "Ministry" of many believers will be revealed as a means to further their own personal aspiration of wealth and fame rather than bringing Glory to the Lord. Everything that is hidden now will be brought to light before our Lord (see Jeremiah 17:10).

Now is the time all Christians should be living their lives in view of the Judgement Seat of Christ and the rewards (Crowns) that can be earned for their faithful lives. Jesus warned us ahead of time that many will try to take these crowns from the Believers:

> *"Behold, I come quickly: hold that fast which thou hast, that no man take thy crown."* (Revelation 3:11)

## 5 CROWNS

Jesus was telling his Church to hold on to that *"which thou hast"* so that it would not lose their Crowns. The Word of God shows there are 5 different Crowns that are possible for Christians to earn. All Christians should be earnestly striving for these rewards so they may cast them unto Jesus in the very near future:

> *"The four and twenty elders fall before him that sat on the throne and worship him that liveth forever and ever, and **cast their crowns before the throne**, saying, "Thou art worthy, 0 Lord, to receive glory and honor and power: for thou hast created all things, and for thy pleasure they are and were created."* (Revelation 4:10-11)

What a glorious day that will be when we are able to worship our great God! Will you have crowns to lay at His feet? Let's see what the 5 possible Crowns are and how they can be obtained.

## CROWN OF LIFE

> *"Blessed is the man that endureth temptation: for when he is tried, he shall receive the **crown of life**, which the Lord hath promised to them that love him."* (James 1:12)

The Crown of Life is the first and basic crown. It is given to those Christians who truly love Jesus. Because they love Him, they are faithful to Him. When trials and tests arrive in their life, they remain true to Him. They are overcomers who endure temptations and win this crown for remaining faithful to Jesus.

## INCORUPTIBLE CROWN

> *"Know ye not that they which run in a race run all, but one receiveth the prize? So run, that ye may obtain. And every*

> *man that striveth for the mastery is temperate in all things. Now they do it to obtain a corruptible crown; but we an **incorruptible**. I therefore so run... But I keep my body and bring it into subjection...lest I be a castaway."*
> (I Corinthians 9:24-25)

The Incorruptible Crown is awarded to the Christian who wins the spiritual race that is set before each believer. It is a daily race in which the sins of the flesh must be put off by allowing the Holy Spirit to take control. It is not won until the race is over, and even Apostle Paul was concerned that he might not win this prize. Yes, even Paul was concerned that he might be a castaway. This should be a lesson for everyone who says it doesn't matter how you live after you are saved. Even the great Apostle Paul was concerned for his own life.

To win this crown, the believer must be successful in *"crucifying the flesh"* as is described in Galatians 5:16, 19-26, and by turning from the things of this world.

# CROWN OF RIGHTEOUSNESS

> *"I have fought a good fight, I have finished my course, I have kept the faith: Henceforth there is laid up for me a **crown of righteousness**, which the Lord, the righteous Judge, shall give me at that day: and not to me only but unto all them also that love his appearing."* (II Tim. 4:7-8)

The Crown of Righteousness is the next level of reward. It is given for keeping the true faith, ie., keeping God's Word. Directly associated with keeping the faith is *"loving his appearing"*. Living in the Endtime, you would think that all Christians would receive this crown. And yet, very few modern day Christians even care to discuss the return of the Lord. Paul is saying that those Christians who are alert to and anxiously looking for the Lord to return are the ones who are keeping the faith. Those who long for that great day are given the wonderful promise of receiving the Crown of Righteousness.

**CROWN OF REJOICING**

> *"For what is our hope, or joy, or **crown of rejoicing**? Are not even ye in the presence of our Lord Jesus Christ at his Coming? For ye are our glory and joy."*
> (I Thessalonians 2:19-20)

The last two crowns are the highest rewards of the five crowns. The Crown of Rejoicing is also known as the soul winner's crown. In the above verse, Paul was referring to the very faithful Christians from Thessalonica. Paul was instrumental in helping them become faithful Christians who were counted worthy of entering the Kingdom. Because of this, they are seen as Holy evidence before Jesus Christ at His return. Their faithfulness to this high calling provided their entrance into the Kingdom, and, as a result, Paul saw their faithful lives as a Crown of Rejoicing when the Lord returns.

Likewise, those Christians who teach others and lead others into a deeper relationship with Jesus will also receive the Crown of Rejoicing when the Lord comes. While winning people into a saving knowledge of Christ is important, this crown is given to those who are actually helping other Christians become faithful disciples. Solomon put it this way:

> *"...he who wins souls is wise."* (Proverbs 11:30)

## CROWN OF GLORY

*"Be shepherds of God's flock that tis under your care, serving as overseers, not because you must, but because you are willing, as God wants you to be; not greedy for money but eager to serve; not lording it over those entrusted to you, but being examples to the flock. And when the Chief Shepherd appears you will receive the **crown of glory** that will never fade away."* (I Peter 5:2-4)

The Crown of Glory is given to the faithful under-shepherd who properly feeds the sheep. It is any Christian who has matured in the faith and who is teaching others the true teachings from the Word of God. When Jesus comes, they will receive the Crown of Glory.

Let briefly review the 5 possible Crowns and how they are earned.

---

### THE 5 CROWNS

**CROWN OF LIFE**
Repent and be baptized. Patiently endure the present trials and testings in life. Die to self.

**INCORRUPTIBLE CROWN**
Be filled with the Spirit. Put off fleshly desires.

**CROWN OF RIGHTEOUSNESS**
Mature in the Word. Keep the faith. Love His appearing.

**CROWN OF REJOICING**
Be a soul winner. Lead other Christians into the deeper relationship with Jesus.

**CROWN OF GLORY**
Know the Scriptures. Nourish the flock of God with the deeper truths from God's Word.

As mentioned earlier, Jesus warned us not to let any man take our crowns. Let's look at each crown, and see how others can make us lose our crowns.

## Crown of Life

The Crown of Life is given to those who patiently endure the present trials and tests that come in this life. Those who are overcomers will receive this crown as a reward for their faithfulness. Others can take this crown from the believer through false teaching. Most of the Church has not been taught what it really means to be an overcomer. By so doing most Christians will not gain this most basic crown.

Most believers feel that they are automatically overcomers by virtue of their salvation. They have never allowed the Holy Spirit to teach them how to really experience His overcoming power in their life. Sadly, false teaching has robbed most of the Church of this most basic reward.

## Incorruptible Crown

The incorruptible crown is given to those faithful believers who allow the Spirit to be the master over their flesh. Others will try to take this crown from you by telling you it doesn't matter how you live after you are saved. They will say, "Go sow a few wild oats," or "You are saved by Grace, don't worry about it."

The worldly Laodicea church age is filled with Christians that have given into the desires of the flesh. Don't listen to them, don't let them take your crown. The small pleasures this world has to offer, pail in comparison to the many astounding things God has awaiting His faithful.

## Crown of Righteousness

This crown is given to those who keep the faith and love His appearing. Others will try to take this crown from you by trying to get you to give up looking for the Lord's return. This can happen in two ways. Most in the Church are not interested in speaking about the Rapture. By so doing, these believers can discourage your faith and hope in the Lord's coming; thereby causing you to lose your crown. The second way is through the many false alarms that have sounded. Don't give up on Jesus! He said He is coming again, and He will return at just the right time, and not one day late! Don't let others take this crown from you.

### Crown of Rejoicing
The soul winners crown is given to those who are actually leading other Christians into a deeper relationship with Jesus. This crown has been stolen from most in Church today because the doctrine of Rewards is not understood or taught. Don't let this keep you from earning this reward. Help others be faithful disciples of Christ.

### Crown of Glory
The Crown of Glory is given to those who are found nourishing God's flock. Others will try to take this crown from you by telling you that it is reserved for the Pastor. Sadly, many Pastors are not properly feeding the flock of God today. This Crown is God's reward to those who know and love God's Word enough to teach others the real truth. Be faithful to Him, and He will give you this reward very, very soon!

All Christians should be actively seeking all of the above crowns. These crowns are rewards for faithfully serving the Lord.

Many Christians will arrive at the Judgement Seat of Christ without even one crown. These Christians will be saved, but they will not receive any rewards due to their unfruitful and unfaithful life. Now is the time to repent, while there is still time!

## Come to Repentance

> "But, beloved, be not ignorant of this one thing, that one day is with the Lord as a thousand years, and a thousand years as one day. The Lord is not slack concerning his promise, as some men count slackness, but is **long-suffering toward us**, not willing that any should perish, but that all should **come to repentance**." (II Peter 3:8-9)

Speaking through the Apostle Peter, the Lord is trying to teach Christians (toward us) a very important lesson. First of all he is admonishing the Church not to be ignorant of one important fact regarding His return. Speaking in the context of the Day of the Lord and the judgement to come, Peter is telling the Church that 1 day to the Lord = 1,000 years.

Students of Bible prophecy are well aware of the importance of this. Hosea's prophecy tells us:

> *"I will go and return to my place...**after two days** will he revive us; in the third day he will raise us up, and we shall live in his sight."* (Hosea 5:15-6:2)

Hosea was speaking of the 2 day period between the $1^{st}$ and $2^{nd}$ comings of the Lord. The Bible quite clearly tells us that there is to be a 2,000 year period between the time Jesus leaves until he returns. This is a very important fact that the Lord does not want His people to be ignorant of. He is trying to tell the Church <u>when</u> He is coming and <u>what they should do</u> before He comes!

Peter plainly tells us we are not to be ignorant of how God measures time. Most Believers have very little interest in the subject of eschatology and they don't want to be around those who discuss a possible timing of when the Lord is going to return. Because of this, many in the Church will completely miss out because of their ignorance to what the Word of God says!

We firmly believe that the Lord is getting ready to return. Before He comes; however, He wants as many Believers as possible to **come to repentance**. If the Believer fails to repent before He returns, the above Scripture indicates that they will "perish." Yes, this verse is telling the Believer that if they fail to come to repentance in time then they will perish! We believe this is further confirmation to the message in this book where we show that there will be a great separation in the body of Christ. Those Firstfruit Believers represented by the wise virgins are looking for the Lord to return and will come to repentance and be ready when He comes. However, the rest of the Church (pictured as foolish virgins) fail to hear the clear warnings given in the Scriptures and

## Preparation For Days Ahead

will perish in the Tribulation period if they fail to come to repentance.

The wise virgins come to the Lord on a regular basis confessing their sins:

> *"If we confess our sins, he is faithful and just to forgive us our sins, and to cleanse us from all unrighteousness."*
>
> (I John 1:9)

By keeping short accounts before the Lord, the Bride's wedding garment is kept clean and spotless:

> *(25) Husbands, love your wives, even as Christ also loved the church, and gave himself for it; (26) That he might sanctify and cleanse it with the **washing of water by the word,** (27) That he might present it to himself a glorious church, **not having spot, or wrinkle, or any such thing**; but that it should be **holy and without blemish.**"*
>
> (Ephesians 5:25-27)

The process of sanctification comes about by a daily washing by the word that allows the Holy Sprit to point out areas that need cleansing. The wise virgins then humbly come to the Lord asking for forgiveness that can only be provided by the precious blood of our Lord and Saviour Jesus Christ.

Are your wedding garments spotted today? Have the cares of this world, the pride of life and the lusts of the flesh caused your wedding gown to become soiled? Now is the time to come to the Lord and make sure your life is without spot or wrinkle. The Bride of Christ is living the holy and blameless life separated from the darkness of this dying world. She longs to be with her Bridegroom and wants to make sure she is ready whenever He may arrive.

**We cry out to the Church today: Repent, Jesus is coming back again very soon! Make sure you are really ready to meet the Bridegroom!**

Greatest Revival in History

The Word of God records one of the greatest revivals in all of history in the 3$^{rd}$ chapter of the book of Jonah. Notice why this revival occurred:

*"And the word of the LORD came unto Jonah the second time, saying, Arise, go unto Nineveh, that great city, and preach unto it the preaching that I bid thee. So Jonah arose, and went unto Nineveh, according to the word of the LORD. Now Nineveh was an exceeding great city of three days' journey. And Jonah began to enter into the city a day's journey, and **he cried**, and said, **Yet forty days, and Nineveh shall be overthrown**. <u>**So the people of Nineveh believed God, and proclaimed a fast, and put on sackcloth, from the greatest of them even to the least of them.**</u> For word came unto the king of Nineveh, and he arose from his throne, and he laid his robe from him, and covered [him] with sackcloth, and sat in ashes. And he caused [it] to be proclaimed and published through Nineveh by the decree of the king and his nobles, saying, Let neither man nor beast, herd nor flock, taste any thing: let them not feed, nor drink water. But let man and beast be covered with sackcloth, and <u>**cry mightily unto God**</u>: yea, <u>**let them turn every one from his evil way, and from the violence that [is] in their hands**</u>. Who can tell [if] God will turn and repent, and turn away from his fierce anger, that we perish not? <u>**And God saw their works, that they turned from their evil way;**</u> and God repented of the evil, that he had said that he would do unto them; and he did [it] not"* (Jonah 3:1-10).

Notice that Jonah warned the great city of Nineveh that God was going to bring Judgment if they failed to repent. But the people of Nineveh believed God, and as a result, they cried out to God in true repentance. God saw this true repentance by the fact that they all turned from their evil ways and because of this, He did not destroy the city. This story shows that one of the greatest revivals in all of history took place when the people **listened** to **God** and **believed** Him. They got serious with God and true repentance was the result.

Like Jonah, we believe God has given us an important message to deliver to the Church. The Word of God says that Jesus is coming back after 2,000 years, but before He returns He wants all Believers to come to repentance. Yes, he wants Christians to repent and to turn from our wicked ways.

> *"If my people, who are called by my name, will humble themselves and pray and seek my face and **turn from their wicked ways**, then will I hear from heaven and will forgive their sin and will heal their land"* (II Chronicles 7:14).

**Please, please, please....listen to the message God has in His Word. This is not some message we have made up. This message comes directly from God's Holy Word.**

Blameless – Counted Worthy
Finally, let's see how Peter ends his 2nd letter of admonition to the Church:

> *"Wherefore, beloved, seeing that ye look for such things, **be diligent** that ye may be found of him in peace, **without spot**, and **blameless**..." "Ye therefore, beloved, seeing that ye know these things before, beware lest ye also, being led away with the error of the wicked, fall from your own steadfastness. But grow in the grace and in the knowledge of our Lord and Savior, Jesus Christ..."*
> (II Peter 3:14, 17-18).

Peter reminds us that we diligently need to continue to be found blameless and without spot. This reminds us of the promise found in Daniel 12:9-10: *"And he said, Go thy way, Daniel: for the words are closed up and sealed till the time of the end. **Many** shall be **purified**, and made white, and tried; but the wicked shall do wickedly: and none of the wicked shall understand; but the **wise** shall **understand**.*" Peter rightly warns the Believer to continue to be diligent so we may be found blameless and Daniel confirms that those who are wise will understand. As a result of reading this book, we hope it will motivate many Christians to examine their lives now to make sure they are truly ready for what lies ahead. It is our hearts desire that this book will result in many appearing before the Judgement Seat of Christ and receiving all of the five crowns discussed earlier. By faithfully living a life that is pleasing to the Lord and continuing in the Lord's service until He returns, may he find each of us diligently striving to delight Him in order to hear Him say:

> "*Well done, thou good and faithful servant... enter into the joy of thy Lord*" (Matthew 25: 21).

As we approach the time of our Lord's return, our prayer is that the Church will heed the warnings given in this book. May all Believers come to true repentance and turn from our wicked ways and continue to pray the Lord counts us worthy to escape the coming Tribulation period that is about to ensnare this world. Jesus in coming very soon and we need to get ready and wake up the rest of the Church before it is too late! And let us never forget the prayer for watchfulness that our Lord instructed us to pray:

*"And take heed to yourselves, lest at any time your hearts be overcharged with surfeiting, and drunkenness, and cares of this life, and so that day come upon you unawares. For like a snare shall it come on all them that dwell on the face of the whole earth.* **Watch ye, therefore, and <u>pray always</u>, that ye may be <u>accounted worthy to escape</u> all these things that shall come to pass, and to stand before the Son of Man"** (Luke 21:34-36).

# Epilogue

When I started writing this book, it began as another article for our newsletter ***Prophecy Countdown***. I had no idea when I started what the Lord planned for me to write; but once I began, He continued to reveal new discoveries I had never seen.

It certainly was not my intent for this study to become another attempt at setting a date for the Lord's return. The Church has witnessed enough of these over the years, but time is running out and the Lord's return can not be too far off.

Whenever possible dates are discussed, the scoffers rise to the surface; and if we were living in biblical times, they would probably be the first ones to cast the stones. While writing this book may prompt many with the desire to cast a stone my way, it will be worth it if just one soul turns their life around and begins living for Jesus. If just one Christian comes to know Him as their wonderful Bridegroom it will be worth it all.

The Church is at the threshold of time when the last grains of sand in the hour glass are about to descend. Jesus Christ is getting ready to return for His faithful Bride who is looking and longing to be with her Bridegroom. Our prayer is that this book will force many to examine their life now before the darkness of the Tribulation hour engulfs this planet. The time of testing that lies ahead is very real, but Jesus gave us the promise that those *"counted worthy"* will be able to escape. May this book awaken many to the lateness of the hour and motivate multitudes to become overcomers:

> *"(5) He that **overcometh**, the same shall be **clothed in white raiment**; and I will not blot out his name out of **the book of life**, but I will confess his name before my Father, and before his angels."* (Revelation 3:5)

# Reference Notes

Chapter 4
1) The Blindness that exists over Israel is beautifully described by the Apostle Paul as a veil that covers their hearts:

> *"(14) But their minds were made dull, for to this day the same **veil remains when the old covenant is read.** It has not been removed, because **only in Christ is it taken away.** (15) Even to this day when Moses is read, **a veil covers their hearts.** (16) But whenever anyone turns to the Lord, **the veil is taken away.** (17) Now the Lord is the Spirit, and where the Spirit of the Lord is, there is freedom. (18) And **we, who with unveiled faces all reflect the Lord's glory**, are being transformed into his likeness with ever increasing glory, which comes from the Lord, who is the Spirit."*
> (II Corinthians 3:14-18 – NIV)

Chapter 5
2) Luke 21:28 *"Now, when these things are beginning to take place, be elated and lift up your heads, because your deliverance is imminent"* **The New Testament – An Expanded Translation**
by Kenneth S. Wuest

Chapter 6
3) Recommended books on God's Feast Days:
Michael Strassfeld's: **Jewish Holidays**
Lyn Mize's: **The Open Door**
www.ffruits.org/firstfruits/sevenfeasts
Peggy Flowers:***Will The Real Rapture Feast Please Stand Up?***
(i.e. Pentecost = Rapture Feast)

4) The Counts at the top of Page 64 were adapted from: www.tribulationperiod.com   PROPHECY UPDATE NUMBER 102, January 10, 2003 by Pastor Tom McElmurry. Tom is one of very few Pastors who hold to the view of a 3 ½ year Tribulation period and we are grateful for his insight into this subject.

### Chapter 8

5) ***Prophecy in the News*** is a ministry headed by J.R. Church and Gary Stearman. They produce this exceptional monthly prophecy magazine. For more information, their website can be found at: www.prophecyinthenews.com

6) An excellent online Study Bible can be found at: www.blueletterbible.org/index.html This is one of the best on-line Bible sites for serious Bible students.

### Chapter 9

7) Colin Deal's book entitled: ***The Great Tribulation – How Long?*** has a very good description of the Abomination of Desolation occurring when Jerusalem is surrounded:

> "What then is the **abomination of desolation**? …it is simply when Gentile armies commit abomination by marching against, and desolating, the city (Jerusalem) where God chose to place His name." (Page 50)

### Chapter 10

8) Tim McHyde's book: ***Know the Future*** discusses Planet X in great detail. We caution the reader that Tim believes in a Post-Tribulation Rapture, but some of his writings are very interesting. While we disagree with many of the writings in his book, he does have curious ideas but many incorrect interpretations. www.EscapeAllTheseThings.com

### Chapter 11

9) The Desolation of Daniel 9:27, as described by Tom McElmurry (See # 4 above): "Daniel's clock stopped ticking when Christ was crucified. Christ confirmed the covenant at his baptism, then he set out to fulfill its promises to Abraham, Isaac, Jacob, and David in the final 70th week. But he was cut off (crucified)… and at this point the clock stopped when he made the temple spiritually desolate, thereby causing the acceptance of the sacrifice and the oblation to cease being acceptable to God. And it will continue to be so **until the consummation of this age** when he returns and, at that time, **the spiritually desolate will have his wrath poured upon them.**"

# Reference Notes

> *"And he shall confirm the covenant with many for one week: and in the midst of the week he shall cause the sacrifice and the oblation to cease, and for the overspreading of abominations he shall make it desolate, even until the consummation, and that determined shall be poured upon the desolate"* **(Daniel 9:27)**
>
> *"O Jerusalem, Jerusalem, thou that killest the prophets, and stonest them which are sent unto thee, how often would I have gathered thy children together, even as a hen gathereth her chickens under her wings, and ye would not! [38] Behold, your house is left unto you desolate. [39] For I say unto you, Ye shall not see me henceforth, till ye shall say, Blessed is he that cometh in the name of the Lord."* **(Matthew 23:37-39)**

Dave Watchman also wrote on this subject in an article entitled ***The Truth of Daniel 9:27***. He notes that the error began in 1885 when the "Revised Version" (R.V.), was recommended to be the replacement for the Authorized King James Bible by the so called "textual critics" of that era!" He then compares the purified Authorized Version (A.V.) with the corrupted Revised Version (R.V.) which renders Daniel 9:27 falsely. The R.V. "makes" the "he" - the Antichrist, compared to the purified A.V. text which declares the "he" to be Jesus Christ:

| Authorized King James Bible | The Revised Version of 1885 |
|---|---|
| And he shall confirm the covenant with many for one week: and in the midst of the week he shall cause the sacrifice and the oblation to cease, and for the overspreading of abominations he shall make it desolate, even until the consummation, and that determined shall be poured upon the desolate. | And he shall make a firm covenant with many for one week: and for the half of the week he shall cause the sacrifice and the oblation to cease: and upon the wing of abominations shall come one that maketh desolate; and even unto the consummation, and that determined, shall wrath be poured out upon the desolator. |

"...the A.V. says "*and he* (Jesus) *shall confirm* (strengthen) *the covenant* (referring to the Abrahamic covenant already mentioned in Dan. 9:4, Gen. 12:1-3) *with many for one week* (7-years), whereas the R.V. says And "he" (Antichrist) will make a firm covenant (peace) with many for one week (7-years)."

His article goes on to point out that Sir Robert Anderson and C.I. Scofield were close friends who used the false rendering brought out by the Revised Version in their classic works: ***The Coming Prince*** and the ***Scofield Bible***. "As time went on, other writers such as Larkin, Ironside, McClain, Pentecost, Green, Walvoord, etc. wrote prophetic books which "also agreed" with Sir Robert's R.V. interpretation of Daniel 9:27 and formed the basis of our modern prophetic teachings we hear today!"

The modern interpretation believed and taught by the majority of the Church today has its roots in this change made to God's Word in 1885.

<u>Chapter 12</u>

10) Lyn Mize's article on the ***Ten Virgins*** has an excellent explanation for Matthew 25:5 found at:

> www.ffruits.org/firstfruits/tenvirginsarticle.aspx

The following is a brief excerpt from this article:

> *"While the bridegroom tarried, they all slumbered (3573) and slept."* (Matthew 25:5)

"This verse has been grossly mistranslated, and the translation is misleading. This parable thus far has provided two antithetical groups of people (i.e., wise and foolish virgins). There is a difference in the reactions between the wise and the foolish virgins. The antithesis continues in this verse, but the translators failed to see this. A correct paraphrase of this verse...is as follows: (Mat. 25:5 LMP) *While the Bridegroom tarried in His coming, all of the ten virgins* **either beckoned for him to return** *or* **they fell asleep**.

## Reference Notes

An accurate, literal word-for-word translation of this verse is as follows: (Mat. 25:5 LMV) *While the bridegroom tarried, they all beckoned or slept.*

The Greek word that has been translated slumbered literally means to nod in signaling or beckoning for what one desires to be done.

The five wise virgins are beckoning for Jesus to return, but the five foolish virgins have fallen asleep. This is precisely the situation in the Church today. The Philadelphia church is wide awake signaling, praying, beckoning, pleading for Jesus to return, but the remainder of the Church is fast asleep, and oblivious to the signs of the times. The word "maranatha" is a beckon for Jesus to return."

Other Recommended Books and Websites:
While the following websites still teach a 7 Year Tribulation period, they are excellent websites that understand the coming Separation (Firstfruits Rapture of those who are ready and counted worthy followed by the Main Harvest Rapture of the Church later on):

**The Open Door**
by Lyn Mize             www.ffruits.org

**The Bride of Christ**
by Pastor Randy Shupe   www.pastorrandyshupe.com

**Reflections of His Image**
by Nancy Missler        www.kingshighway.org

**Rapture – A Reward for Readiness**
by Dr. Ray Brubaker     www.godsnews.com

# Appendix A

## Sign of Christ's Coming

April 8, 1997

**Comet Hale-Bopp Over New York City**
**Credit and Copyright:** J. Sivo
http://antwrp.gsfc.nasa.gov/apod/ap970408.html

"What's that point of light above the World Trade Center? It's Comet Hale-Bopp! Both faster than a speeding bullet and able to "leap" tall buildings in its single orbit, Comet Hale-Bopp is also bright enough to be seen even over the glowing lights of one of the world's premier cities. In the foreground lies the East River, while much of New York City's Lower Manhattan can be seen between the river and the comet."

**"As it was in the days of Noah, so it will be at the coming of the Son of Man."** (Matthew 24:37)

These words from our wonderful Lord have several applications about the Tribulation period that is about to ensnare this world.

Seas Lifted Up
Throughout the Old Testament, the time of the coming Tribulation period is described as the time when the "seas have lifted up" and also as coming in as a "flood" (please see Jeremiah 51:42, Hosea 5:10, Daniel 11:40 and Psalm 93:3-4 for just a few examples).

This is a direct parallel to the time of Noah when the Great Flood of water came to wipe out every living creature except for righteous Noah and his family and the pairs of animals God spared. While God said He would never flood the earth again with water, the coming Judgement will be by fire (II Peter 3:10). The book of Revelation shows that approximately three billion people will perish in the terrible time that lies ahead (see Revelation 6:8 and 9:15).

2 Witnesses
A guiding principle of God is to establish a matter based upon the witness of 2 or more:

> "...a matter must be established by the testimony of two or three witnesses" (Deuteronomy 19:15)

In 1994, God was able to get the attention of mankind when Comet Shoemaker-Levy crashed into Jupiter on the 9$^{th}$ of Av (on the Jewish calendar). Interestingly, this Comet was named after the "two" witnesses that first discovered it.

In 1995, "two" more astronomers also discovered another comet. It was called Comet Hale-Bopp, and it reached its closest approach to planet Earth on March 23, 1997. It has been labeled as the most widely viewed comet in the history of mankind.

Scientists have determined that Comet Hale-Bopp's orbit brought it to our solar system 4,465 years ago (see Notes 1 and 2 below). In other words, the comet made its appearance near Earth in 1997 and also in 2468 BC. Remarkably, this comet preceded the Great

Flood by 120 years! God warned Noah of this in Genesis 6:3:

> *"My Spirit shall not strive with man forever, for he is indeed flesh; yet his days shall be one hundred and twenty years."*

Days of Noah
What does all of this have to do with the Lord's return? Noah was born around 2948 BC, and Genesis 7:11, tells us that the Flood took place when Noah was 600, or in 2348 BC.

Remember, our Lord told us: **"As it was in the days of Noah, so it will be at the coming of the Son of Man." (Matthew 24:37)**

In the original Greek, it is saying: *"exactly like"* it was, so it will be when He comes (see Strong's #5618).

During the days of Noah, Comet Hale-Bopp arrived on the scene as a harbinger of the Great Flood. Just as this same comet appeared before the Flood, could its arrival again in 1997, be a sign that God's final Judgement, also known as the time of Jacob's Trouble, is about to begin?

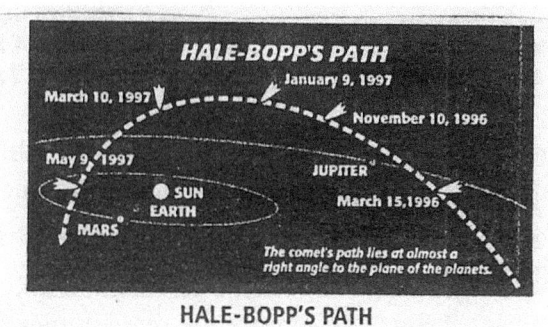

HALE-BOPP'S PATH

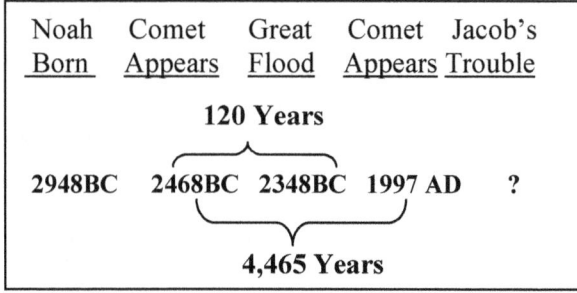

Comet Hale-Bopp's arrived 120 years before the Flood as a warning to mankind. Only righteous Noah heeded God's warning and built the ark as God instructed. By faith Noah was obedient to God and, as a result, saved himself and his family from destruction.

Remember, Jesus told us His return would be preceded by great heavenly signs:

*"And there shall be signs in the sun, and in the moon, and in the stars; and upon the earth distress of nations, with perplexity; the sea and the waves roaring."* (Luke 21:25)

Just as this large comet appeared as a 120 year warning to Noah, its arrival in 1997, tells us that Jesus is getting ready to return again. Is this the **"Sign"** Jesus referred to?

> Jesus was asked 3 questions by the disciples:
> *"Tell us, (1) when shall these things be (the destruction of the city of Jerusalem), and (2) what shall be the **sign** of thy coming, and (3) of the end of the world?"* (Matthew 24:3)

## Sign of Christ's Coming

The **first** question had to do with events that were fulfilled in 70 AD. The **third** question has to do with the future time at the very end of the age.

The **second** question, however, has to do with the time of Christ's second coming. Jesus answered this second question in His description of the days of Noah found in Matthew 24:33-39:

> *(33) "So likewise ye, when ye shall see all these things, know that it is near, [even] at the doors. (34) Verily I say unto you, This generation shall not pass, till all these things be fulfilled. (35) Heaven and earth shall pass away, but my words shall not pass away. (36) But of that day and hour knoweth no man, no, not the angels of heaven, but my*

## Appendix A - Sign of Christ's Coming

> *Father only.* <sup>(37)</sup> ***But as the days of Noe [were], so shall also the coming of the Son of man be.*** <sup>(38)</sup> *For as in the days that were before the flood they were eating and drinking, marrying and giving in marriage, until the day that Noe entered into the ark,* <sup>(39)</sup> *And knew not until the flood came, and took them all away; so shall also the coming of the Son of man be."*

Jesus is telling us that the **sign** of His coming will be as it was during the days of Noah. As Comet Hale-Bopp was a sign to the people in Noah's day, its arrival in 1997, is a sign that Jesus is coming back again soon. Comet Hale-Bopp could be the very sign Jesus was referring to which would announce His return for His faithful.

Remember, Jesus said, *"**exactly** as it was in the days of Noah, so will it be when He returns."* The appearance of Comet Hale-Bopp in 1997, is a strong indication that the Tribulation period is about to begin, but before then, Jesus is coming for His Bride!

**Keep looking up! Jesus is coming again very soon!**

As Noah prepared for the destruction God warned him about 120 years before the Flood, Jesus has given mankind a final warning that the Tribulation period is about to begin. The horrible destruction on 9/11, is only a precursor of what is about to take place on planet Earth. We need to be wise like Noah and prepare for the time ahead. Always remember our Lord's instructions:

### Watch and Pray

> "And take heed to yourselves, lest at any time your hearts be overcharged with surfeiting, and drunkenness, and cares of this life, and so that day come upon you unawares. For like a snare shall it come on all them that dwell on the face of the whole earth. **Watch ye, therefore, and pray always, that ye may be accounted worthy to escape all these things that shall come to pass, and to stand before the Son of Man**" (Luke 21:34-36).

## Footnotes

(1) The original orbit of Comet Hale-Bopp was calculated to be approximately 265 years by engineer George Sanctuary in his article: ***Three Craters In Israel***, published on March 31, 2001 that can be found at:

http://www.gsanctuary.com/3craters.html#3c_r13

Comet Hale-Bopp's orbit around the time of the Flood changed from 265 years to about 4,200 years. Because the plane of the comet's orbit is perpendicular to the earth's orbital plane (ecliptic), Mr. Sanctuary noted: "A negative time increment was used for this simulation...to back the comet away from the earth.... past Jupiter... and then out of the solar system. The simulation suggests that the past-past orbit had a very eccentric orbit with a period of only 265 years. When the comet passed Jupiter (***around 2203BC***) its orbit was deflected upward, coming down near the earth 15 months later, with the comet's period changed from 265 years to about (***4,200***) years (***added text*** *to article for clarity*)...

(2) Don Yeomans, with NASA's Jet Propulsion Laboratory made the following observations regarding the comet's orbit: "By integrating the above orbit forward and backward in time until the comet leaves the planetary system and then referring the osculating orbital elements...the following orbital periods result:

Original orbital period before entering planetary system = 4200 years Future orbital period after exiting planetary system = 2380 years." This analysis can be found at: http://www2.jpl.nasa.gov/comet/ephemjpl6.html

---

Based upon the above two calculations we have the following:

$265^{(a)} + 4,200^{(b)} = 4,465$ Years

1997 AD – 4,465 Years = 2468 BC = Year Hale Bopp arrived

(a) Orbit period calculated by George Sanctuary before deflection around 2203 BC
(b) Orbit period calculated by Don Yeomans after 1997 visit

# Appendix B

***Of the Prophecy of the Seventy Weeks.*** *By Sir Isaac Newton*

The Vision of the Image composed of four Metals was given first to *Nebuchadnezzar*, and then to *Daniel* in a dream: and *Daniel* began then to be celebrated for revealing of secrets, *Ezek.* xxviii. 3. The Vision of the four Beasts, and of *the Son of man* coming in the clouds of heaven, was also given to *Daniel* in a dream. That of the Ram and the He-Goat appeared to him in the day time, when he was by the bank of the river *Ulay*; and was explained to him by the prophetic Angel *Gabriel*. It concerns the *Prince of the host*, and the *Prince of Princes*: and now in the first year of *Darius* the *Mede* over *Babylon*, the same prophetic Angel appears to *Daniel* again, and explains to him what is meant by the *Son of man*, by the *Prince of the host*, and the *Prince of Princes*. The Prophecy of the *Son of man* coming in the clouds of heaven relates to the second coming of *Christ*; that of the *Prince of the host* relates to his first coming: and this Prophecy of the *Messiah*, in explaining them, relates to both comings, and assigns the times thereof.

This Prophecy, like all the rest of *Daniel*'s, consists of two parts, an introductory Prophecy and an explanation thereof; the whole I thus translate and interpret.

> [1] '*Seventy weeks are* [2] *cut out upon thy people, and upon thy holy city, to finish transgression, and* [3] *to make an end of sins, to expiate iniquity, and to bring in everlasting righteousness, to consummate the Vision and* [4] *the Prophet, and to anoint the most Holy.*
>
> '*Know also and understand, that from the going forth of the commandment to cause to return and to build* Jerusalem, *unto* [5] *the Anointed the Prince, shall be seven weeks.*

> 'Yet threescore and two weeks shall [6] it return, and the street be built and the wall; but in troublesome times: and after the threescore and two weeks, the Anointed shall be cut off, and [6] it shall not be his; but the people of a Prince to come shall destroy the city and the sanctuary: and the end thereof shall be with a flood, and unto the end of the war, desolations are determined.
>
> 'Yet shall he confirm the covenant with many for one week: and in half a week he shall cause the sacrifice and oblation to cease: and upon a wing of abominations he shall make it desolate, even until the consummation, and that which is determined be poured upon the desolate.'

*Seventy weeks are cut out upon thy people, and upon thy holy city, to finish transgression*, &c. Here, by putting a week for seven years, are reckoned 490 years from the time that the dispersed *Jews* should be re-incorporated into [7] a people and a holy city, until the death and resurrection of *Christ*; whereby *transgression should be finished, and sins ended, iniquity be expiated, and everlasting righteousness brought in, and this Vision be accomplished, and the Prophet consummated*, that Prophet whom the *Jews* expected; and whereby *the most Holy* should be *anointed*, he who is therefore in the next words called the *Anointed*, that is, the *Messiah*, or the *Christ*. For by joining the accomplishment of the vision with the expiation of sins, the 490 years are ended with the death of *Christ*. Now the dispersed *Jews* became a people and city when they first returned into a polity or body politick; and this was in the seventh year of *Artaxerxes Longimanus*, when *Ezra* returned with a body of *Jews* from captivity, and revived the *Jewish* worship; and by the King's commission created Magistrates in all the land, to judge and govern the people according to the laws of God and the King, *Ezra* vii. 25. There were but two returns from captivity, *Zerubbabel*'s and *Ezra*'s; in *Zerubbabel*'s they had only commission to build the Temple, in *Ezra*'s they first became a polity or city by a government of their own. Now the years of this *Artaxerxes* began about two or three months after the summer solstice, and his

## Appendix B – Of the Prophecy of the 70 Weeks

seventh year fell in with the third year of the eightieth *Olympiad*; and the latter part thereof, wherein *Ezra* went up to *Jerusalem*, was in the year of the *Julian Period* 4257. **Count the time from thence to the death of *Christ*, and you will find it just 490 years.(a)** If you count in *Judaic* years commencing in autumn, and date the reckoning from the first autumn after *Ezra*'s coming to *Jerusalem*, when he put the King's decree in execution; the death of *Christ* will fall on the year of the *Julian Period 4747, Anno Domini* 34 **(b)** and the weeks will be *Judaic* weeks, ending with sabbatical years; and this I take to be the truth: but if you had rather place the death of *Christ* in the year before, as is commonly done, you may take the year of *Ezra*'s journey into the reckoning.

**(a) 4257 BC to 32 AD = 490 Years**

**(b) Should be 4745 or 32 AD**

*Know also and understand, that from the going forth of the commandment to cause to return and to build* Jerusalem, *unto the Anointed the Prince, shall be seven weeks*. The former part of the Prophecy related to the first coming of *Christ*, being dated to his coming as a Prophet; this being dated to his coming to be Prince or King, seems to relate to his second coming. There, the Prophet was consummate, and the most holy anointed: here, he that was anointed comes to be Prince and to reign. For *Daniel*'s Prophecies reach to the end of the world; and there is scarce a Prophecy in the Old Testament concerning *Christ*, which doth not in something or other relate to his second coming. If divers of the ancients, as [8] *Irenæus*, [9] *Julius Africanus*, *Hippolytus* the martyr, and *Apollinaris* Bishop of *Laodicea*, applied the half week to the times of *Antichrist*; why may not we, by the same liberty of interpretation, apply the seven weeks to the time when *Antichrist* shall be destroyed by the brightness of *Christ*'s coming?

The *Israelites* in the days of the ancient Prophets, when the ten Tribes were led into captivity, expected a double return; and that at the first the *Jews* should build a new Temple inferior to *Solomon*'s, until the time of that age should be fulfilled; and afterwards they should return from all places of their captivity, and build *Jerusalem* and the Temple gloriously, *Tobit* xiv. 4, 5, 6: and to express the glory and excellence of this city, it is figuratively said to be built of precious stones, *Tobit* xiii. 16, 17, 18. *Isa.* liv. 11, 12. *Rev.* xi. and called the *New Jerusalem*, the *Heavenly Jerusalem*, the *Holy City*, the *Lamb's Wife*, the *City of the Great King*, the *City into which the Kings of the earth do bring their glory and honor*.

*Now* while such a return from captivity was the expectation of *Israel*, even before the times of *Daniel*, I know not why *Daniel* should omit it in his Prophecy. This part of the Prophecy being therefore not yet fulfilled, I shall not attempt a particular interpretation of it, but content myself with observing, that as the <u>**seventy**</u> and the <u>***sixty two weeks***</u> were ***Jewish*** weeks, **ending with sabbatical years;** so the <u>***seven weeks***</u> are the compass of a ***Jubilee***, and begin and end with actions proper for a *Jubilee*, and of the highest nature for which a *Jubilee* can be kept: and that since *the* **commandment to return and to build** Jerusalem, <u>**precedes the Messiah the Prince 49 years**</u>; it may perhaps come forth not from the *Jews* themselves, but from some other kingdom friendly to them, and precede their return from captivity, and give occasion to it; and lastly, that this rebuilding of *Jerusalem* and the waste places of *Judah* is predicted in *Micah* vii. 11. *Amos* ix. 11, 14. *Ezek.* xxxvi. 33, 35, 36, 38. *Isa.* liv. 3, 11, 12. lv. 12. lxi. 4. lxv. 18, 21,22. and *Tobit* xiv. 5. and that the return from captivity and coming of the *Messiah* and his kingdom are described in *Daniel* vii. *Rev.* xix. *Acts* i. *Mat.* xxiv. *Joel* iii. *Ezek.* xxxvi. xxxvii. *Isa.* lx. lxii. lxiii. lxv. and lxvi. and many other places of scripture. The manner I know not. **Let time be the Interpreter.**

*Yet* **threescore and two weeks** *shall it return, and the street be built and the wall, but in troublesome times: and* **after the threescore and two weeks** *the* **Messiah shall be cut off,** *and it shall not be his; but the people of a Prince to come shall destroy the city and the sanctuary.*

## Appendix B – Of the Prophecy of the 70 Weeks 133

Having foretold **both comings of *Christ***, and dated the last from their returning and building *Jerusalem*; to prevent the applying that to the building *Jerusalem* by *Nehemiah*, he distinguishes this from that, by saying that from this period to the *Anointed* shall be, **not seven weeks**, but **threescore and two weeks,** and this not in prosperous but in troublesome times; and at the end of these Weeks the *Messiah* shall not be the Prince of the *Jews*, but be cut off; and *Jerusalem* not be his, but the city and sanctuary be destroyed. Now *Nehemiah* came to *Jerusalem* in the 20th year of this same *Artaxerxes*, while *Ezra* still continued there, *Nehem.* xii. 36, and found the city lying waste, and the houses and wall unbuilt, *Nehem.* ii. 17. vii. 4, and finished the wall the 25th day of the month *Elul, Nehem.* vi. 15, in the 28th year of the King, that is, in *September* in the year of the *Julian Period* 4278. **Count now from this year threescore and two weeks of years, that is 434 years,** and the reckoning will end in *September* in the year **of the *Julian Period* 4712** which is the year in which **Christ was born,(c) 3 BC** according to *Clemens Alexandrinus*, *Irenæus*, *Eusebius*, *Epiphanius*, *Jerome*, *Orosius*, *Cassiodorus*, and other ancients; and this was the general opinion, till *Dionysius Exiguus* invented the vulgar account, in which *Christ*'s birth is placed two years later. If with some you reckon that *Christ* was born three or four years before the vulgar account, yet his birth will fall in the latter part of the last week, which is enough. How after these weeks *Christ* was cut off and the city and sanctuary destroyed by the *Romans*, is well known. **(c) 4278 BC to 3 BC = 434 Years (62 x 7)**

*Yet shall he confirm the covenant with many for one week.* He kept it, notwithstanding his death, till the rejection of the *Jews*, and calling of *Cornelius* and the *Gentiles* in the seventh year after his passion. **(Unorthodox interpretation???)**

*And in half a week he shall cause the sacrifice and oblation to cease*; that is, by the war of the *Romans* upon the *Jews*: which war, after some commotions, began in the 13th year of *Nero*, **A.D. 67,** in the spring, when *Vespasian* with an army invaded them; and ended in the second year of *Vespasian*, **A.D. 70,** in the autumn,

*Sept.* 7, when *Titus* took the city, having burnt the Temple 27 days before: so that it **lasted three years and an half.** *And upon a wing of abominations he shall cause desolation, even until the consummation, and that which is determined be poured upon the desolate.* The Prophets, in representing kingdoms by Beasts and Birds, put their wings stretch out over any country for their armies sent out to invade and rule over that country. Hence a wing of abominations is an army of false Gods: for an abomination is often put in scripture for a false God; as where *Chemosh* is called [10] the abomination of *Moab*, and *Molech* the abomination of *Ammon.* **The meaning therefore is, that the people of a Prince to come shall destroy the sanctuary, and abolish the daily worship of the true God, and overspread the land with an army of false gods**; and by setting up their dominion and worship, cause desolation to the *Jews*, until the times of the *Gentiles* be fulfilled. For *Christ* tells us, that the abomination of desolation spoken of by *Daniel* was to be set up in the times of the *Roman Empire*, *Matthew*. xxiv. 15.

Thus have we in this short Prophecy, a prediction of all the main periods relating to the coming of the *Messiah*; **the time of his birth, that of his death, that of the rejection of the *Jews*,** the **duration of the *Jewish* war** whereby he caused **the city and sanctuary to be destroyed,** and the **time of his second coming**: and so the interpretation here given is more full and complete and adequate to the design, than if we should restrain it to his first coming only, as Interpreters usually do.

**We avoid also the doing violence to the language of *Daniel*,** by taking the **_seven weeks_** and **_sixty two weeks_** for one number. Had that been *Daniel*'s meaning, he would have said **_sixty and nine weeks,_** and **not** *seven weeks* and *sixty two weeks*, **a way of numbering used by no nation.** In our way the years are *Jewish Luni-solar years,* [11] as they ought to be; and the *seventy weeks of years* are *Jewish weeks* ending with *sabbatical years*, which is very remarkable. For **they end either** with the **year of the birth** of *Christ*, two years before the vulgar account, or with the **year of his**

**death**, or with the seventh year after it: all which are *sabbatical years*. Others either count by Lunar years, or by weeks not *Judaic*: and, which is worst, they ground their interpretations on erroneous Chronology, excepting the opinion of *Funccius* about the *seventy weeks*, which is the same with ours. For they place *Ezra* and *Nehemiah* in the reign of *rtaxerxes Mnemon*, and the building of the Temple in the reign of *Darius Nothus*, and date the weeks of *Daniel* from those two reigns.

**NOTES:**

**(a) 4257 BC to 32 AD = 490 Years**
**(b) 4745 = 32 AD (not 4747 or 34 AD)**
**(c) 4278 BC to 3 BC = 434 Years (62 x 7)**

---

Regarding Newton's perception of how God was working in the lives of men in revealing truths from the Word of God, Newton wrote:

> "Amongst the Interpreters of the last age there is scarce one of note who hath not made some discovery worth knowing: and thence I seem to gather that God is about opening these mysteries. The success of others put me upon considering it; and if I have done any thing which may be useful to following writers, I have my design."

While Newton is well known for his many contributions to math and science, his contribution to the study of the Word of God may have been his greatest accomplishment.

# Appendix C – Outline of Book of Revelation

**INTRODUCTION** (1:1-20)
1. Introduction and benediction (1-3)
   **("Blessing" promised for reading & following)**
2. Greetings to the seven churches of Asia (4-6)
3. Announcement of Christ's coming (7)
4. The Lord's self-designation (8)

I. <u>**A GENERAL OVERVIEW OF THE CONFLICT**</u> (1:9-11:19)
A. **VISION OF CHRIST AMONG THE LAMPSTANDS** (1:9-20)

B. **LETTERS TO THE SEVEN CHURCHES** (2:1-3:22)
1. The church at Ephesus (2:1-7)
2. The church at Smyrna (2:8-11)
3. The church at Pergamos (2:12-17)
4. The church at Thyatira (2:18-29)
5. The church at **Sardis** (3:1-6) – **Few found Worthy**
6. The church at **Philadelphia** (3:7-13)
   **Promised Escape from Tribulation** (praying Luke 21:36)
7. The church at Laodicea (3:14-22)
   **Lukewarm** (spewed out into Tribulation unless they repent)

C. **THE THRONE SCENE** (4:1-5:11)
1. God on the throne (4:1-11)
2. The Lamb worthy to open the seven-sealed scroll (5:1-14)

D. <u>**THE OPENING OF THE "7" SEALS**</u> (6:1-8:1)
1. <u>**First seal**</u>: The white horse and its rider (6:1-2)
2. <u>**Second seal**</u>: The red horse and its rider (6:3-4)
3. <u>**Third seal**</u>: The black horse and its rider (6:5-6)
4. <u>**Fourth seal**</u>: The pale horse and its rider(s) (6:7-8)
5. <u>**Fifth seal**</u>: The martyrs under the altar (6:9-11)
6. <u>**Sixth seal:**</u> Cataclysmic disturbances (6:12-17)
   **GOD'S WRATH COMING (see Revelation 16:1 below)**
7. <u>**Interlude:**</u> Sealing of the 144,000 on earth, and the great Multitude in heaven (7:1-17)
8. <u>**Seventh seal**</u>: Silence in heaven (8:1) – **GOD'S WRATH (see Rev. 16:1 below)**

E. **THE SOUNDING OF "7" TRUMPETS** (8:2-11:19)

## Seven angels prepare to sound their trumpets (8:2-6)
1. **First** trumpet: Third of vegetation destroyed (8:7)
2. **Second** trumpet: Third of **sea** creatures/ships destroyed (8:8-9)
3. **Third** trumpet: Third of **rivers** & springs become bitter, many men die (8:10-11)
4. **Fourth** trumpet: Third of **sun**, moon, and stars struck, affecting day & night (8:12)
   **Three-fold woe announced (8:13)**
5. **Fifth** trumpet (**first woe**): Locusts from bottomless pit torment men **5 months** (9:1-12)
6. **Sixth** trumpet (**second woe**): Four angels with an army of two hundred million, killing a third of mankind (9:13-21)
   **Another interlude (10:1-11:14)**
   a. The angel with the little book (10:1-11)
   b. The two witnesses (11:1-13)
7. **Seventh** trumpet (**third woe**): Victory of Christ & His kingdom proclaimed (11:14-19) *"In a moment, in the twinkling of an eye, at the **last trump**..., and we shall be changed."*
   (I Corinthians 15:52)

> "And I heard a great voice out of the temple saying to the **seven angels**, Go your ways, and **pour out the vials of the wrath of God** upon the earth." (Revelation 16:1)

| | | |
|---|---|---|
| Rev 11:3 | 2 Witnesses Prophesy | **1,260 days** |
| Rev 11:7 | Killed by Anti-Christ | |
| Rev 11:11 | Resurrection after 3 days | |
| | (2nd Woe is Past - Rev. 11:14) | |
| Rev 12:6 | Israel in Wilderness | **1,260 days** |
| Rev 12:1 | Israel in Wilderness | **3 1/2 Years** |
| Rev 13 | Anti-Christ has Power | **42 Months** |

## F. **THE "7" BOWLS OF WRATH** (15:1-16:21)
Prelude to pouring out the **seven bowls of wrath** (15:1-8)
1. **First bowl**: Sores on those who worshipped the beast and his image (16:1-2)
2. **Second bowl: Sea** turns to blood, all sea creatures die (16:3)
3. **Third bowl: Rivers** and springs turn to blood (16:4-7)
4. **Fourth bowl**: Men are scorched by the **sun** (16:8-9)
5. **Fifth bowl: Pain and darkness upon the beast** and his kingdom (16:10-11)
6. **Sixth bowl**: Euphrates dried up, three unclean spirits gather the kingdoms of the earth for the **battle at Armageddon** (16:12-16)
7. **Seventh bowl**: Great earthquake, the great city divided, Babylon is remembered, cataclysmic events (16:17-21)

++++++++++++++++++++++++++++++++++++++++++++++

## II. **A CLOSER LOOK AT THE CONFLICT** (12:1-22:5)

### A. THE GREAT CONFLICT (12:1-14:20)
1. The Woman, the Child, the Dragon, and the rest of the Woman's offspring (12:1-17)
2. The beast from the sea (13:1-10)
3. The beast from the land (13:11-18)
4. The Lamb and the 144,000 on Mount Zion (14:1-5)
5. Proclamations of six angels (14:1-20) (Summary of 6 visions)
   See Chapter 5 of *The Coming Spiritual Earthquake* at:
   www.ProphecyCountdown.com
6. Reaping the earth's harvest, and the grapes of wrath (14:14-20)

### B. **THE FALL OF BABYLON, THE HARLOT** (17:1-19:10)
1. The scarlet woman and the scarlet beast (17:1-6)
2. The mystery of the woman and beast explained (17:7-18)
3. The fall of Babylon the great proclaimed and mourned (18:1-24)
4. The exaltation in heaven over the fall of the great harlot (19:1-5)
5. The announcement of the marriage supper of the Lamb (19:6-10)

C. **THE DEFEAT OF THE LAMB'S ENEMIES** (19:11-20:15)
1. Christ the victorious warrior and King of Kings (19:11-16)
2. **The beast**, his armies, and the false prophet (land beast) are **defeated** (19:17-21)
3. Satan is bound for a thousand years, while those martyred reign with Christ (20:1-6)
4. Satan released to deceive the nations once more, but is finally defeated once for all (20:7-10)
5. The final judgment (20:11-15)

D. **THE ETERNAL DESTINY OF THE REDEEMED** (21:1-22:5)
1. The new heaven & new earth, New Jerusalem, God dwelling with His people (21:1-8)
2. The New Jerusalem described (21:9-27)
3. The water of life, the tree of life, and the throne of God and the Lamb (22:1-5)

**CONCLUSION** (22:6-21)
1. The time is near, do not seal up the book (22:6-11)
2. The testimony of Jesus, the Spirit, and the bride (22:12-17)
3. Warning not to tamper with the book, and closing prayers (22:18-21)

Note: This Outline is an adaptation of a similar one found at: www.blueletterbible.org with notes and comments made by the author. Also please note that a blessing is promised to those who read and follow its instructions (Revelation 1:1-3).

# Appendix D – Watching for Jesus

*"So Christ was once offered to bear the sins of many;* **and unto them that look for him shall he appear the second time** *without sin unto salvation."* (Hebrews 9:28)

The Word of God says that Jesus is returning the second time to those who are looking for him to return. Are you looking for Jesus to come again? If not, now is the time to start your watch because it is much later than most people think.

We do not know for certain the exact time that Jesus will return. Just before Jesus left this earth the first time he told His disciples that He was going to return and He commanded them to "Watch". What does it mean to continue watching?

Some of the things *"Watching"* entails include:

1) Being aware of the prophetic signs in God's Word.
2) Living a life of Holiness before our Lord.
3) Living a life separated from the world.
4) Encouraging one another with the wonderful Hope of His soon return.
5) Telling others Jesus is coming soon and their need to be ready.
6) Praying the prayer Jesus taught us to pray in Luke 21:

*"And take heed to yourselves, lest at any time your hearts be overcharged with surfeiting, and drunkenness, and cares of this life, and so that day come upon you unawares. For like a snare shall it come on all them that dwell on the face of the whole earth.* **Watch** *ye, therefore, and* **pray always***, that ye may be accounted worthy to escape all these things that shall come to pass, and to stand before the Son of Man"* (Luke 21:34-36).

The act of *"Watching"* is serious business with our Lord. If we fail to continue our diligence, Revelation 3:3, gives us fair warning:

> *"Remember therefore how thou hast received and heard, and hold fast, and repent. If therefore **thou shalt not watch, I will come on thee as a thief,** and thou **shalt not know** what hour I will come upon thee."* (Revelation 3:3)

Those who are not *"Watching"* will be taken by surprise since a thief comes unannounced. The Wise and Faithful followers of Jesus, however, will continue *"Watching"* for Him and they will not be surprised. Begin *"Watching"* today before it is too late! Jesus is Coming, Very, Very Soon!

Please visit our Website: www.ProphecyCountdown.com for any possible updates to this book to help you continue in your personal *"Watch."*

## Appendix E - GOD'S FEAST DAYS

| FEAST | 2007 | 2008 | 2009 | 2010 | 2011 | 2012 | 2013 | 2014 | 2015 | 2016 | 2017 |
|---|---|---|---|---|---|---|---|---|---|---|---|
| Rosh Hashana | 5768 | 5769 | 5770 | 5771 | 5772 | 5773 | 5774 | 5775 | 5776 | 5777 | 5778 |
| **Purim** | 3/4 | 3/21 | 3/10 | 2/28 | 3/20 | 3/8 | 2/24 | 3/16 | 3/5 | 3/24 | 3/12 |
| **Passover** | | | | | | | | | | | |
| Pesach I | 4/3 | 4/20 | 4/9 | 3/30 | 4/19 | 4/7 | 3/26 | 4/15 | 4/4 | 4/23 | 4/11 |
| Pesach VIII | 4/10 | 4/27 | 4/16 | 4/6 | 4/26 | 4/14 | 4/2 | 4/22 | 4/11 | 4/30 | 4/18 |
| **Pentecost** | 5/27 | 6/15 | 5/31 | 5/23 | 6/12 | 5/27 | 5/19 | 6/8 | 5/24 | 6/12 | 6/4 |
| Tish'a B'Av | 7/24 | 8/10 | 7/30 | 7/20 | 8/9 | 7/29 | 7/16 | 8/5 | 7/26 | 8/14 | 8/1 |
| 10th of Av | 7/25 | 8/11 | 7/31 | 7/21 | 8/10 | 7/30 | 7/17 | 8/6 | 7/27 | 8/15 | 8/2 |
| Eve Rosh Hashana | 9/12 | 9/29 | 9/18 | 9/8 | 9/28 | 9/16 | 9/4 | 9/24 | 9/13 | 10/2 | 9/20 |
| Rosh Hashana | 9/13 | 9/30 | 9/19 | 9/9 | 9/29 | 9/17 | 9/5 | 9/25 | 9/14 | 10/3 | 9/21 |
| Rosh Hashana II | 9/14 | 10/1 | 9/20 | 9/10 | 9/30 | 9/18 | 9/6 | 9/26 | 9/15 | 10/4 | 9/22 |
| **Yom Kippur** | 9/22 | 10/9 | 9/28 | 9/18 | 10/8 | 9/26 | 9/14 | 10/4 | 9/23 | 10/12 | 9/30 |
| **Tabernacles** | | | | | | | | | | | |
| Sukkot I | 9/27 | 10/14 | 10/3 | 9/23 | 10/13 | 10/1 | 9/19 | 10/9 | 9/28 | 10/17 | 10/5 |
| Sukkot II | 9/28 | 10/15 | 10/4 | 9/24 | 10/14 | 10/2 | 9/20 | 10/10 | 9/29 | 10/18 | 10/6 |
| Shmini Atzeret | 10/4 | 10/21 | 10/10 | 9/30 | 10/20 | 10/8 | 9/26 | 10/16 | 10/5 | 10/24 | 10/12 |
| **Feastival of Lights** | | | | | | | | | | | |
| 1 Candle | 12/4 | 12/21 | 12/11 | 12/1 | 12/20 | 12/8 | 11/27 | 12/16 | 12/6 | 12/24 | 12/12 |
| 8 Candles | 12/11 | 12/28 | 12/18 | 12/8 | 12/27 | 12/15 | 12/4 | 12/23 | 12/13 | 12/31 | 12/19 |
| 8th Day Hanukah | 12/12 | 12/29 | 12/19 | 12/9 | 12/28 | 12/16 | 12/5 | 12/24 | 12/14 | 1/1 | 12/20 |

The above Feast Days are provided for the reader to develop their own Timelines for years not covered by this book if needed.

# CHARTS

# 1 – Endtime Calculations Length of Generation
# 2 – Endtime Timeline: 2009-2012
# 3 – Endtime Timeline: 2012-2015
# 4 – Endtime Timeline: 2009-2015
# 5 – Endtime Timeline: 2008-2011
# 6 – Endtime Timeline: 2014-2017

As stated in this book, the purpose of these **Endtime Timelines** is NOT to set EXACT dates for any Endtime events. However, once these Endtime events are set in motion, the final count of days have been given to us in both the books of Daniel and Revelation. We also need to remember that we **are living** in the *"time of the end"* and that the prophecies in Daniel are to be *"unsealed"* at that time and that the *"wise will understand."*

This study examined the periods from 2007 to 2017, and the above Charts #2, #3, and #4, revealed a correlation between the Feast of Pentecost and the Feast of Atonement. These Charts extend out to 2015 as the end of the Tribulation Period and the only period beyond this time that was not included in this book was for the period from 2014 to 2017.

While **Endtime Timelines** could be developed for each of the years, we have decided to include only two additional timelines: Charts # 5 and # 6.

Chart # 5 – Timeline for 2008 to 2011
Chart # 5 is included because it assumes the $42^{nd}$ Year begins one year earlier than what was shown in Chart # 2. Interestingly, June $7^{th}$ 2008 will be the $42^{nd}$ birthday from the time the Old City of Jerusalem was recovered. Pentecost in 2008 falls on June $15^{th}$ 2008, eight days after the generation turns 42. As was discussed in Chapter 5, the number 42 is a highly significant number relating to

the timing for the return of the Lord. Chart # 5 could be the correct Endtime Timeline and Jesus could return for His faithful in 2008.

Chart # 6 – Timeline for 2014 to 2017
Chart # 6 is also included because it assumes the Second Coming could occur 50 years after the recovery of Jerusalem. Fifty is the year of Jubilee, so Chart # 6 could be the correct interpretation.

As Newton reminded us, "Let time be the interpreter." Appendix E is provided for those Watchmen who may want to develop any additional Timelines not covered by this study.

The point is, the purpose of this study was not to set an exact date for the Rapture or the Second Coming of Jesus Christ. We do not know for certain and that is why the wise and faithful will continue "Watching" until that great day arrives.

> *"And take heed to yourselves, lest at any time your hearts be overcharged with surfeiting and drunkenness, and cares of this life, and so that day come upon you unawares. For as a snare shall it come on all them that dwell on the face of the whole earth.* **Watch** *ye therefore, and* ***pray always****, that ye* ***may be accounted worthy to escape*** *all these things that shall come to pass, and to stand before the Son of man."* (Luke 21:34-36)

---

**Note to Readers:** Due to size limitations created by printing parameters, the Charts in the book are not as large as desired. To view and print full color 8 ½ x 11 versions of these Charts please visit: www.ProphecyCountdown.com

User Name: **Luke**
Password:  **2136**

Or send your request for a PDF version of these Charts to:
JimHarmanCPA@aol.com

## ENDTIME CALCULATIONS — CHART # 1
### Length of Generation

| Ministry of Jesus - 3 Scenarios Examined: | ① | ② | ③ |
|---|---|---|---|
| Length of Christ's Ministry (a) | 1,185 | 1,260 | 1,335 |
| Jesus Died (Ended Sacrifices & Offerings) (b) <br> (Daniel 9:26 & 27) | 04/09/32 | 04/09/32 | 04/09/32 |
| Jesus' Ministry Began <br> ((b) - (a)) | 01/09/29 | 10/26/28 | 08/12/28 |

| Length of the Generation <br> That Witnessed Destruction of Jerusalem | ① | ② | ③ |
|---|---|---|---|
| Jesus' Ministry Began (from Above) | 01/09/29 | 10/26/28 | 08/12/28 |
| Temple Destroyed (c) <br> (Matthew 24:2) | 08/05/70 | 08/05/70 | 08/05/70 |
| Number of Days | 15,184 | 15,259 | 15,334 |
| Number of Years | 42 | 42 | 42 |

| The Generation That Will <br> Witness the Return of Messiah | ① | ② | ③ |
|---|---|---|---|
| Recovered Jerusalem (d) <br> (Luke 21:7 & 24) | 6/7/1967 | 6/7/1967 | 6/7/1967 |
| Length of Generation (from Above) <br> (Matthew 24:34 & Luke 21:32) | 15,184 | 15,259 | 15,334 |
| Time to Re-start Daniel's Clock ? (e) <br> (Daniel 9:27 - Resumed) | 1/1/2009 | 3/17/2009 | 5/31/2009 |

(a) Number of days are estimated possible scenarios. Exact length is not known.
(b) Crucifixion of Jesus took place on Wednesday during Passion Week in 32 A.D.
 First half of Daniel's 70th Week ended (Dan. 9:27) Daniel's Clock stopped ticking.
(c) The Temple was destroyed on the 10th of AV in 70 A.D.
(d) The Old City of Jerusalem was recovered by the Jewish people in the 6 day war.
(e) Daniel's Clock stopped when Jesus brought an end to need for sacrifice & offerings.

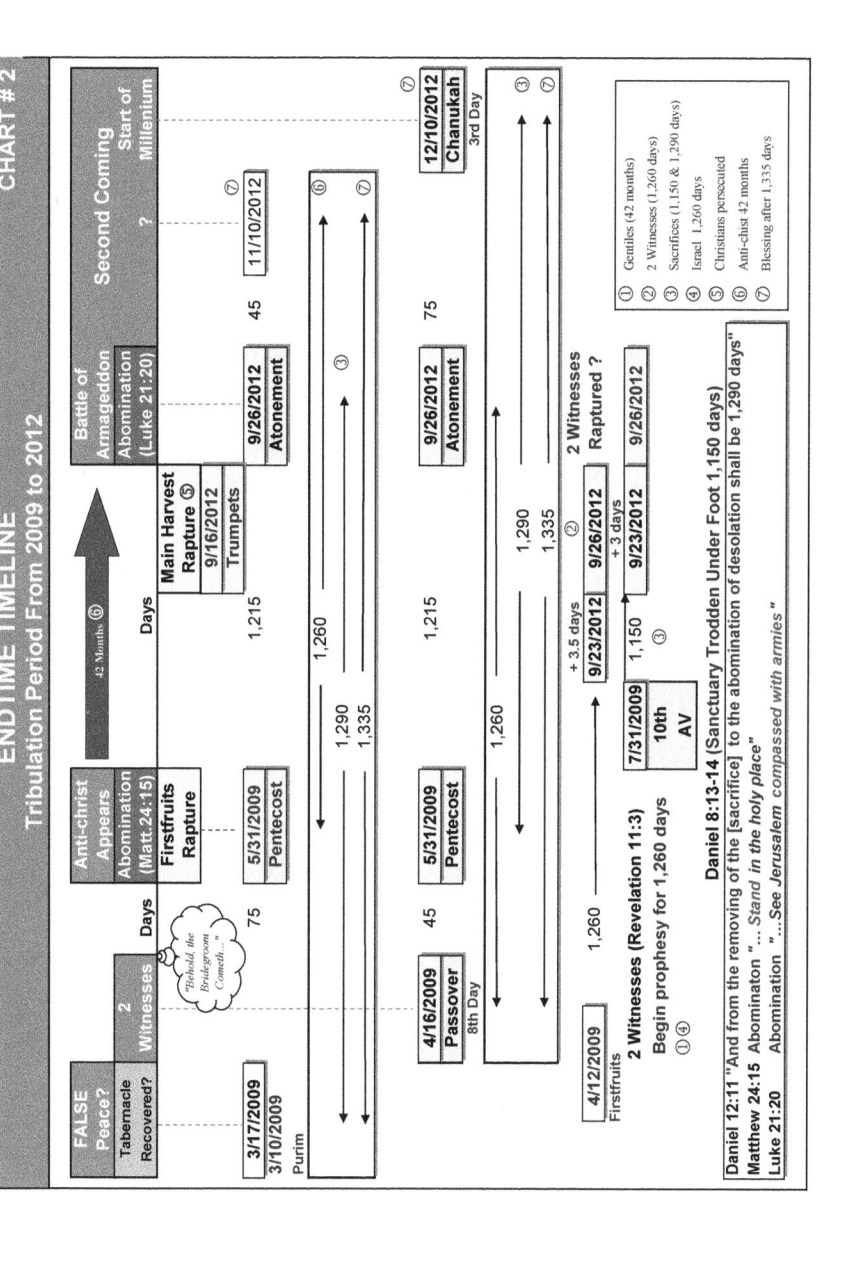

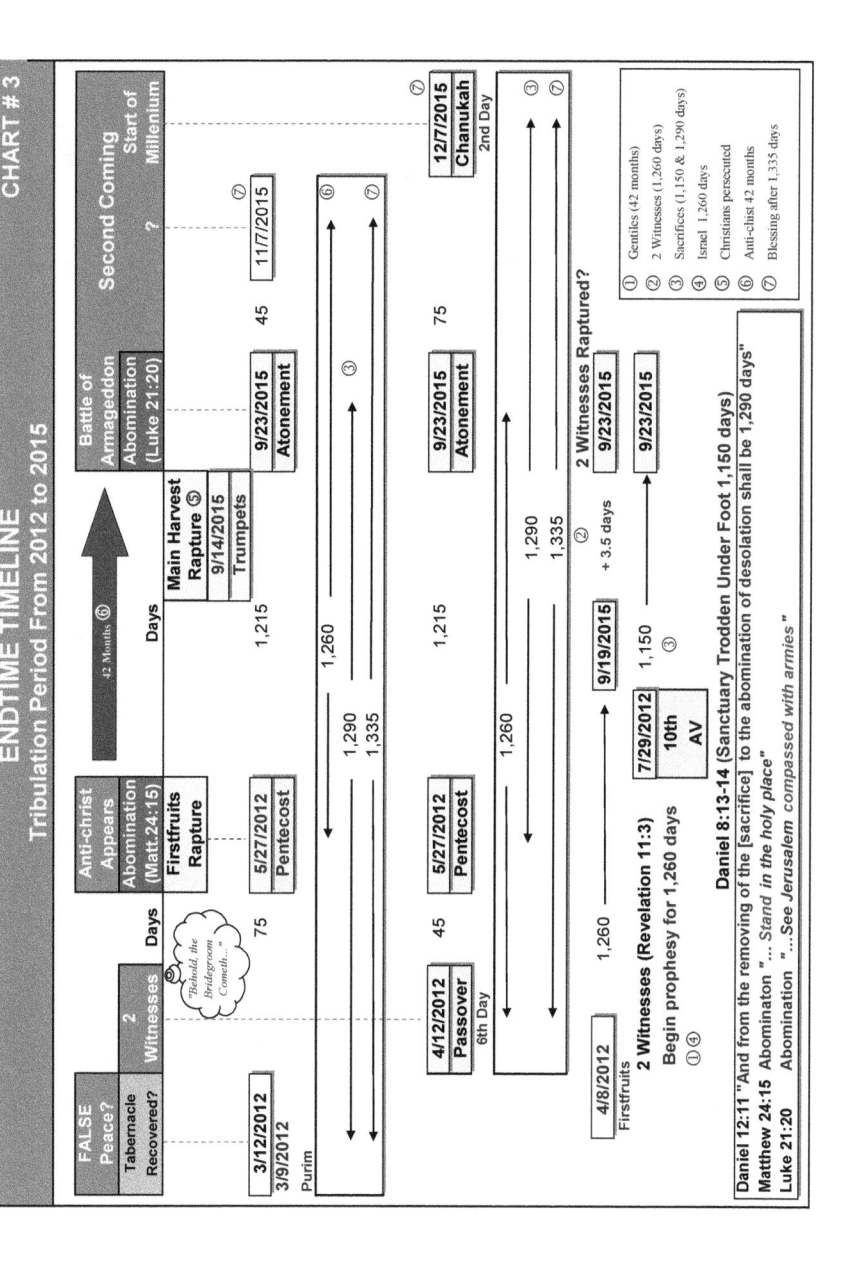

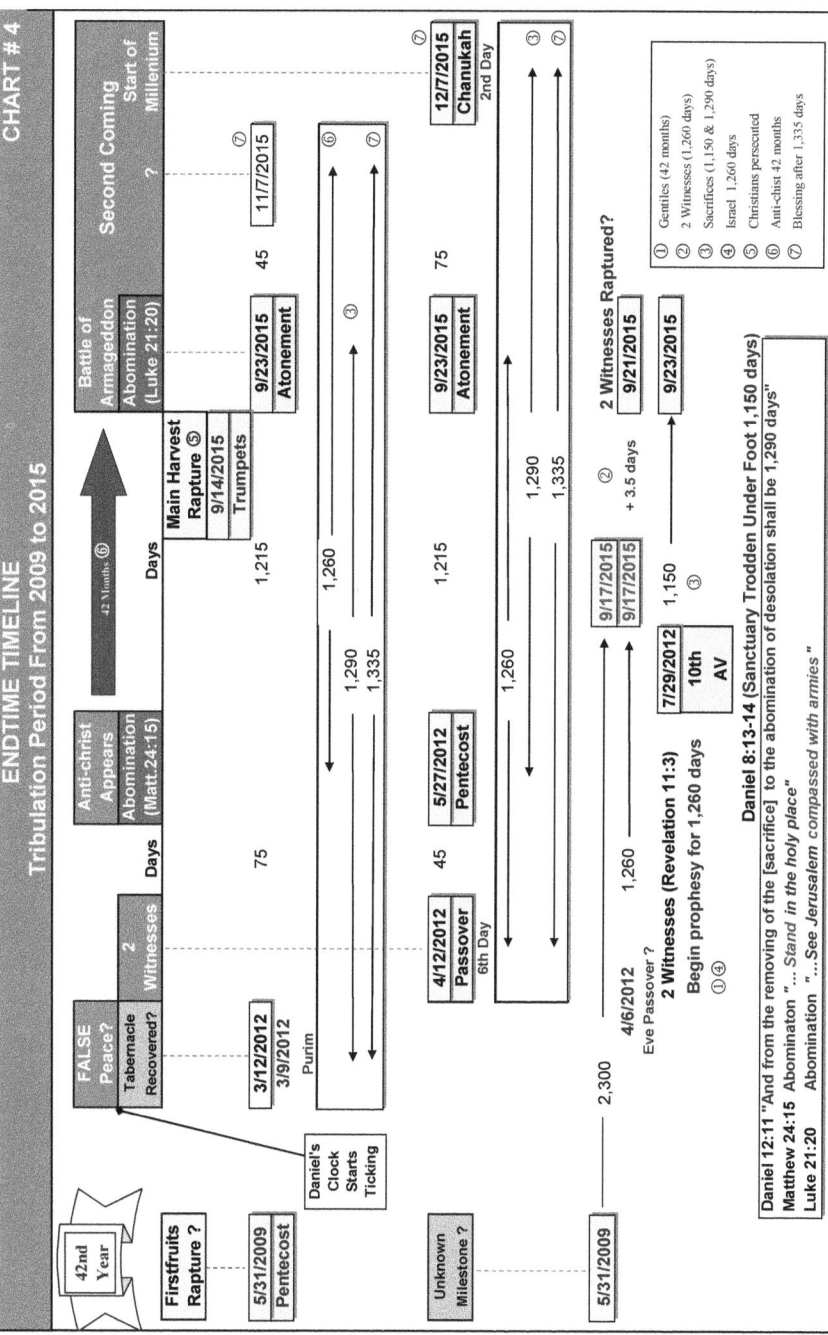

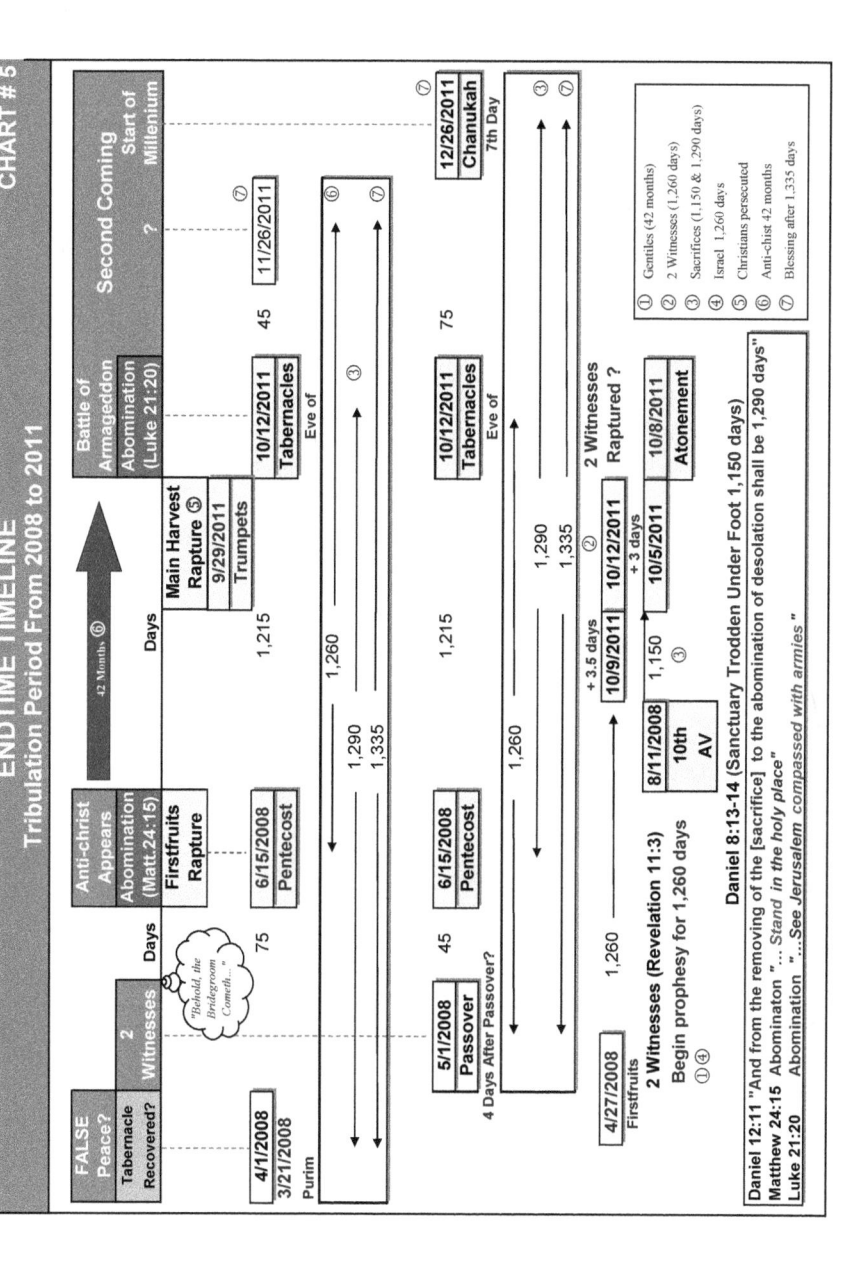

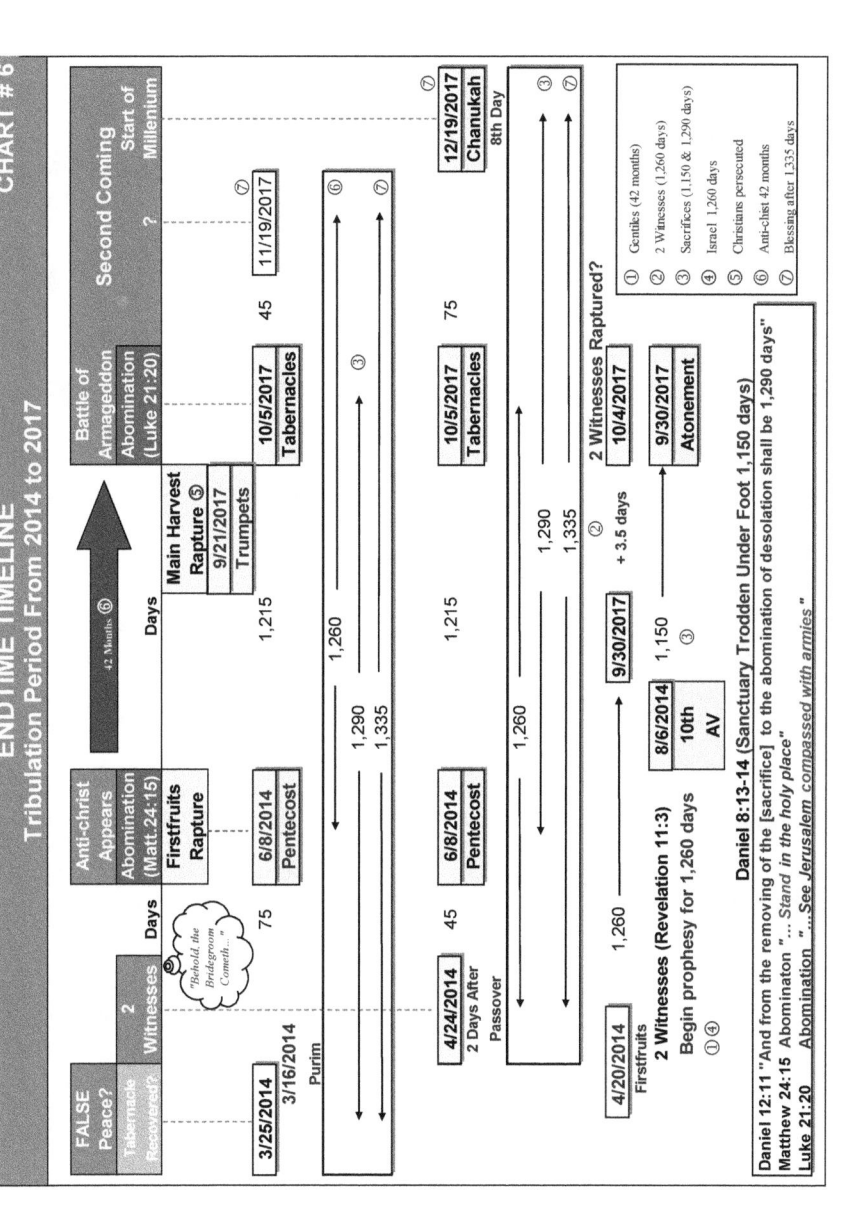

# Special Invitation

This book was written to those who have been saved by Jesus Christ. If you have never been saved before, would you like to be saved? The Bible shows that it's simple to be saved...

- **Realize you are a sinner.**
  *"As it is written, There is none righteous, no, not one:"* Romans 3:10
  *"... for there is no difference. For all have sinned, and come short of the glory of God;"* Romans 3:23

- **Realize you CAN NOT save yourself.**
  *"But we are all as an unclean thing, and all our righteousness are as filthy rags; ..."* Isaiah 64:6
  *"Not by works of righteousness which we have done, but according to his mercy he saved us, ..."* Titus 3:5

- **Realize that Jesus Christ died on the cross to pay for your sins.**
  *"Who his own self bare our sins in his own body on the tree, ..."* I Peter 2:24
  *"... Unto him that loved us, and washed us from our sins in his own blood,"* Revelation 1:5

- **Simply by faith receive Jesus Christ as your personal Savior.**
  *"But as many as received him, to them gave he power to become the sons of God, even to them that believe on his name:"* John 1:12
  *"...Sirs, what must I do to be saved? And they said, Believe on the Lord Jesus Christ, and thou shalt be saved, and thy house."* Acts 16:30,31
  *"...if you confess with your mouth, 'Jesus is Lord,' and believe in your heart God raised him from the dead, you will be saved."* Romans 10:9

**WOULD YOU LIKE TO BE SAVED?**

If you want to be saved, please pray this prayer and mean it with all your heart:

> Lord Jesus, I know that I am a sinner, and unless you save me I am lost forever. I thank you for dying for me at Calvary. By faith I come to you now, Lord the best way I know how, and ask you to save me. I now receive you as my Saviour. In Jesus Christ Name, I pray. Amen.

If you prayed the above prayer you have made the most important decision of your life. You are now saved by the precious blood of Jesus Christ which was shed for you and your sins.

Now that you have prayed to accept Jesus as your personal Saviour you will want to continue to grow in your faith. Find a Church were the Word of God is taught and ask the Holy Spirit to help you as you read the Bible to learn all God has for your life.

Also, go to the Reference section of this book where you will find recommended books and websites that will help you on your wonderful journey.

### **Endtimes**
The Bible indicates that we are living in the final days and Jesus Christ is getting ready to return very soon. This book was written to help Christians prepare for what lies ahead. The Word of God indicates that the Tribulation Period is rapidly approaching and the Antichrist is getting ready to emerge on the world scene.

Jesus promised His disciples that there is a way to escape the horrible time of testing and persecution that will soon devastate this planet.

The whole purpose of this book is to help you get prepared so you won't be left behind when Jesus returns.

# About The Author

Jim Harman has been a Christian for over 30 years. He has diligently studied the Word of God with a particular emphasis on Prophecy. Jim has written several books and his first two books: **The Blessed Hope** and **The Coming Spiritual Earthquake** were widely distributed around the world. They encouraged many to continue *"Looking"* for the Lord's soon return, and brought many to a saving knowledge of Jesus Christ.

Jim's professional experience includes being a Certified Public Accountant (CPA) and a Certified Property Manager (CPM). He has an extensive background in both public accounting and financial management with several well known national firms.

Jim had previously believed in the "Traditional" teaching regarding the *"70$^{th}$ Week of Daniel"* until the Lord showed Him that Jesus Christ fulfilled or will fulfill all of the 9$^{th}$ Chapter of Daniel, and that the Antichrist rendering of Daniel 9:27 is really a grand *"fairy tale"* fostered by the master of deceit and deception: Satan himself.

It is Jim's strong desire that many will come to realize this doctrinal error and begin to appreciate the true message God has for the Church as we approach the final days of this age. Jim believes the Church has learned to apply God's marvelous Grace as a bandage to cover an unclean life and that many Believers need to "Wake-up" to the fact that Jesus Christ is returning for His Holy Bride who is looking and longing to be with her wonderful Bridegroom.

To Contact the Author
For Questions or
To Arrange for
Speaking Engagements:

Jim Harman
P.O. Box 941612
Maitland, FL 32794
JimHarmanCPA@aol.com

---

### ARE YOU A WATCHMAN?

Great Multitudes in our Churches will be going into the Tribulation Period if they Do Not Wake-up!

Help get this message to your friends and loved one while there is still time!

Tell them about this book and website:

www.ProphecyCountdown.com

# THE WATCHMAN
## (Pastors, Teachers, Evangelists and Saints)

> Ezekiel 33
> *¹"A message came to me from the Lord. He said, ²"Son of man, speak to the people of your own country. Tell them, 'Suppose I send enemies against a land. And its people choose one of their men to stand guard. ³He sees the enemies coming against the land. He blows a trumpet to warn the people. ⁴'Someone hears the trumpet. But he does not pay any attention to the warning. The enemies come and kill him. Then what happens to him will be his own fault. ⁵He heard the sound of the trumpet. But he did not pay any attention to the warning. So what happened to him was his own fault. If he had paid attention, he would have saved himself. ⁶'But suppose the guard sees the enemies coming. And he does not blow the trumpet to warn the people. The enemies come and kill one of them. Then his life has been taken away from him because he sinned. But I will hold the guard accountable for his death.' ⁷"Son of man, I have appointed you as a prophet to warn the people of Israel. So listen to my message. Give them a warning from me. ⁸"Suppose I say to a sinful person, 'You can be sure that you will die.' And suppose you do not try to get him to change his ways. Then he will die because he has sinned. And I will hold you accountable for his death. ⁹"But suppose you do warn that sinful person. You tell him to change his ways. But he does not do it. Then he will die because he has sinned. But you will have saved yourself.*

# ARE YOU READY FOR THE WEDDING?

*"The Spirit and the Bride say, Come..."*
(Revelation 22:17)

www.ingramcontent.com/pod-product-compliance
Lightning Source LLC
Chambersburg PA
CBHW060539100426
42743CB00009B/1576